W9-DCN-858

Life as Creation

Life as Creation

A Jewish Way of Thinking about the World

Shalom Freedman

JASON ARONSON INC.
Northvale, New Jersey
London

This book is set in 11 pt. Times by Lind Graphics of Upper Saddle River, New Jersey, and printed by Haddon Craftsmen in Scranton, Pennsylvania.

Copyright © 1993 by Shalom Freedman

10 9 8 7 6 5 4 3 2 1

All rights reserved. Printed in the United States of America. No part of this book may be used or reproduced in any manner whatsoever without written permission from Jason Aronson Inc. except in the case of brief quotations in reviews for inclusion in a magazine, newspaper, or broadcast.

Library of Congress Cataloging-in-Publication Data

Freedman, Shalom.
    Life as creation : a Jewish way of thinking about the world /
Shalom Freedman.
        p. cm.
    ISBN 0-87668-778-8
    1. Creative ability—Religious aspects—Judaism—Quotations,
maxims, etc. 2. Judaism—Quotations, maxims, etc. 3. Creation—
Quotations, maxims, etc. 4. Aphorisms and apothegms. I. Title.
BM645.C73F74 1993
296.3′2—dc20   92-41080

Manufactured in the United States of America. Jason Aronson Inc. offers books and cassettes. For information and catalog write to Jason Aronson Inc., 230 Livingston Street, Northvale, New Jersey 07647.

Contents

Acknowledgments

Hashem has created the world in such a way that most of us come to know in our lives many good people who are of great help to us. I cannot possibly begin to thank all the people from so many different worlds who have been of help to me in the making of this work, so I will mention only a few and ask forgiveness of others who might also have been recalled here. My first and greatest debt is to my parents, Reuben, son of Yehiel Moshe and Sarah Freedman, and Edith, daughter of Chaim and Peshie Zeibert. My father, *zichrono levrachah*, who moved me at an early age to wonder at the meaning of suffering in life, has always been my greatest human inspiration in creation. His everyday speech was a wide-ranging, often heartrending, poetry whose power in feeling lives in me to this day. His dreams for and demands of himself were so great that I have spent more than half a lifetime trying to realize some small part of them. Alongside and helping him always was my mother, the true Jewish mother, who in her love and kindness was the strength of us all. Until her illness took this capacity from her, she was the constant source of help, the one to be turned to no matter how great the problem or difficulty. No matter how many times the world said no to me through the years, she kept faith with me. She is to me the very image of human kindness and goodness.

I also owe a very deep gratitude to my former wife of fourteen years, Luba Freedman. Thanks to her insight into worlds of artistic creation I knew only marginally, my own mental universe was enriched. More important, with her I came to know for the first time the true meaning of love and joy in life. Our children, Yitzhak and Dina — may they live and be well — are God's blessing of those years.

I also must thank my brother, Jake Freedman, and his wife, Sylvia, of Albany, New York. My brother was the strength of my childhood, and he and his wife have been friends of my adult years. Also my sister Joyce Freedman Apsel and her husband, David, must be thanked. My sister's goodness and humorous critical intelligence have been of constant help through the years. Other members of my family have also been of great help to me, most notably my aunts, Molly Zeibert of New York and Lillian (Lakie) Werlin of Troy, New York, and my uncle, Larry Zeibert, of Washington, D. C. Two uncles no longer of this world are proof to me of the truth of our sages, that each and every human being created by God is a unique world of value: Nathan Freedman and Jack Zeibert — may their memories be blessed.

Among many friends from my old world, the United States, I will mention only two: my former mentor at Cornell University, Professor Cushing Strout, who showed me how the life of the mind could be a multidisciplinary adventure in freedom, and Andy Waldman of Ridgewood, New Jersey, a friend since childhood whose kindness and humor have lightened the journey. In Israel, where the list is even longer, I owe a special debt to Rabbi Kadish Waldman. *Hashem* sent him to me at my hour of greatest need, and he helped me as he has helped many others. I also am very grateful to Rabbi Meir Schweiger of Machon Pardes, whose profound teaching of Torah made me better understand how I, after many years of study, have only begun to touch the surface of our great Tradition. Chaim Mayerson, Jerusalem editor and translator, has given me valuable professional advice on a number of occasions. Chaim Pearl, rabbi and author, has been a constant help and inspiration. His wide Jewish knowledge and deep sense of communal responsibility are an example I can only imperfectly emulate. I feel a deep gratitude to Rabbi Henry (Eliahu Chaim) Barneis, of blessed memory, who more than anyone else helped teach me the joy of *mitzvah* in prayer. I cannot forget the late Dr. Yaacov Shapira, engineer-inventor, who from the first greeted a stranger with a welcome countenance and for years helped me feel part of his family. A victim of terrorism, part of his legacy to me is renewed determination to make my own small contribution to the building of the land of Israel he was so devoted to.

A special word of thanks to Arthur Kurzweil and the staff of Jason Aronson Inc. for their help in making a dream of many years come true.

To all these people and the many unnamed others who have put goodness in my life, I dedicate this work. In my heart you are with me, even when you know it not.

May the Holy One, blessed be He, strengthen and sustain us in this life and its redemption in all our worlds to come.

Prayer as Preface

All I am, and all I have, and all I have created, and all I
will create, is from You. I know this work, which is written
in my name, is nothing if it does not serve Your Name. I
prayer that the work I have done here will find favor in
Your sight and will not be seen as arrogance and sin.

You know how from childhood I have struggled to
know the truth of Your world, struggled to understand the
meaning of my life here. You know how I questioned the
suffering of those I loved and how this suffering has led
me to understand that without Your blessing, there is no
ultimate hope for any of us.

You have made me work and wait many years for this
book of thoughts. You have given me, through them and
in the making of them, the joy of revelation, the joy of
creation. They are Your gift to me and hopefully will be
my gift to my readers. I hope they will inspire these readers
to deeper understanding of their place in Your world and
their own power to serve You in creation of their own.

The idea at the center of this work is that You have
commanded us, Your creatures, to walk in Your way and
imitate You through creation of our own. It is that You
have given us the freedom to participate in that creation
that is the historical process of redemption and that You
have chosen Your people for a special role in revealing
Your Name to the world. But every other kind of human

creation, collective or individual, also reflects Your chosenness of us.

I believe I have taken this concept of *creation* and
developed it in ways and worlds that are new. This too is
Your gift to me.

I believe the readers of this work will have a unique
adventure in thought and that many will come across
questions they themselves have often asked and create
answers as new thought of their own. I believe too that
many of the thoughts of this work may come to the readers
as a kind of poetic revelation that will deepen their sense of
the beauty and greatness of Your world.

For those readers who are deep in Torah learning, I
hope the insights presented here will extend and strengthen
their understanding of Your creation. For those Jews on
the outside or margin of understanding of the Tradition, I
hope the thoughts that reveal the special role of the Jewish
people in history will help make for a stronger connection
with our people. I hope too that each and every reader,
especially in reading those chapters on human limitation
and the need for You, will come to understand that
without Your love there is not life for any of us.

As You know, much of this work comes out of my own
years of writing, my thoughts about the process of literary
creation. I suspect here is where I am closest to sinning in
pursuing my own private concerns without special concern
for Your service. Still, You know that often in my literary
work I was striving to help others I love, striving to act as
You have commanded us to act.

I know I am one small creature in a vast universe of
what has gone before and what will come after. I know this
work is one small book among the millions. But You have
given it to me and have chosen me to write it now. I am
thankful for this and pray my readers will have some small
part of the joy of creation in reading this work that I have
had in writing it.

An Additional Word to the Reader

This is a book of thoughts. Each group of thirteen thoughts constitutes a chapter, which is in effect a small essay in itself. The sixty chapters of the work comprise six separate sections: Mankind in Creation, Jewish Creation, God and Creation, Creation and Everyday Moral Life, Creation and the Life of the Mind, and Literary Creation.

The reader can begin anywhere, with any subject or entry that is of interest. But a line of argument does run through the work, and therefore the reader is advised to attempt a consecutive reading. Wisdom literature of this type does not lend itself to swift-paced, once-over-lightly reading. This is the kind of work that challenges the reader to interpretation and rereading. Brief answers on such weighty questions naturally invite both contradiction and an effort by the reader to additional thought. The task of the reader is not necessarily easy. Our father Jacob wrestled with the angel and emerged from this struggle with his truer identity. So may the reader in contending with this work.

I

Mankind in Creation

※   ※   ※

1. AN ESSENTIAL QUALITY OF MANKIND IS THE CAPACITY FOR CREATION

1   The Creator has commanded mankind to walk in the ways of God, i.e., to create in freedom, as God has in creating the world.

2   The creation that has been commanded is cocreation with God, in helping realize the divine plan for the world.

3   The acts of creation, of free decision — which God has commanded — extend into every sphere of human life.

4   There is one realm of creation in which every human being is capable of participating — the realm of moral action in everyday life. And there is another realm, the cultural, in which only a few are chosen as true creators.

5   Creation in the moral realm is walking in God's ways, in doing justice and mercy. And again, this is a kind of human action open to all.

6   In an effort to realize the plan of God, it is possible to understand the whole of human history as a story of human creation.

7   At the very beginning of human history there is Adam's choice in sin, disobedience of God. Mankind subsequently continually struggles against evils it has created for itself by its own power of freedom.

8   The struggle between good and evil, between the creative and destructive, takes place not only as the result of human action in the world, but also within the human heart itself. And yet the test of virtue for the religious Jew is primarily through actions in the world.

9   God's commandment to rule creation is also a commandment to master the powers and forces of nature. Human history can in one sense be studied as man's continual conquest of those powers, either for good or for evil.

10 The capacity to create is the capacity to bring into being that which never existed before. And it is possible that this capacity is so inherent in human nature that human beings are compelled to create, whether they want to or not — just as most people, when they speak, find themselves saying things they never thought of before, whether they want to or not.

11 There is an essential moral distinction between that creation which is made only in service of self and that creation which is understood as work in the service of God.

12 Human history can be understood as that creation which is intended to help complete God's initial

creation of the world. Mankind is therefore cocreator with God in realizing the purpose of human history.

13 If creation is creation of evil as well as of good, the predominant aim of mankind must nonetheless be to help make good predominant in the world.

⬚   ⬚   ⬚

2. MAKING GOODNESS PREDOMINANT IN CREATION

1 God created the world stage by stage, and after each stage He judged this creation as "good."

2 In walking in the ways of righteousness, in doing justice and mercy, mankind helps good predominate in the world.

3 By seeing the good, by recognizing and believing in it, we help create it.

4 Ideally, history and creation should move to higher and higher levels of goodness with each generation. In this way, redemption should come to mankind as the natural consequence of total human effort, generation after generation.

5 But how is it possible to believe that creation is predominantly good in times of evil and suffering, in times of great injustice, in generations in which the world seems by and large lost to evil, in the time before the flood, in the modern era when millions of innocent lives have been taken, and when the innocent

have been tortured and humiliated in ways that made death seem a greater good than life?

6   The choice of good brings more good. The reward of good is greater good. This is essential to the view of the world given by God to the people of Israel.

7   Belief in the predominant goodness of creation means belief that present evil is transient and that, of all evils that have been, there will come a compensation in greater redemption for the injured innocent.

8   A true faith in God's goodness means a belief that even the smallest of our actions for good is not unnoticed and has its own mysterious effect on the whole of creation. And so we are commanded to act for good even in the most minor of our everyday activities.

9   Just as the Creator is fundamentally good, so is the creature made in God's image. Therefore we must always have faith in our own ability to overcome the evil within us.

10   The recurrence of evil generation after generation — the continual presence of the *yetzer hara* within ourselves — raises the question of whether evil is inherent to the process of creation itself, and whether through it comes greater good in the world in the form of the deeper faith of those who sin and then truly repent, through not repeating their action.

11   The human choice of evil — followed by divine intervention, warning punishment, and subsequent human repentance — is the fundamental moral creation drama of mankind.

12   From generation to generation, mankind has become more powerful in its control of nature and has augmented its capacity to recreate the world. But there is no sign that this has led to a corresponding improvement in moral action, to greater goodness.

13   The vision of moral and religious goodness through which God demanded mankind re-create itself was transmitted to the Jewish people.

☒   ☒   ☒

3. CREATION AND CHOSENNESS

1   God chose the Jewish people to impart to mankind the vision of the One Creator God, who demands righteousness and justice of creation.

2   The Jews were not chosen to rule over others or to be worshiped by them. They were chosen to be the messenger of God to mankind and to provide an example, in sacred dedication, of walking in God's ways.

3   The chosenness of the Jews in being commanded to live a life of righteousness is different from other kinds of chosenness in human history. The Jews were chosen by direct revelation for special work of God, while other peoples were chosen indirectly for many other tasks of creation.

4   The chosenness of the Greeks of fifth-century B.C.E. Athens in many fields of human creation is indisputable, as is the chosenness of many other peoples at

many other times. But this type of what might be called *secondary chosenness* is distinct from the primary religious and moral chosenness, the direct chosenness of Israel by God.

5   If all creation is God's, then all creators are in a sense chosen by God, even those who have no intention of serving God directly.

6   The primary, direct supernatural chosenness of the Jews in creation can be compared with the natural chosenness of other peoples and individuals in various times throughout history.

7   In creation, many are called and few are chosen. And this is in all fields and at all levels of life, except the moral.

8   The people we choose to love, and with whom we create our lives, are for us what in a sense mankind is for the Divine Power.

9   Throughout the long stretch of time, many species have striven for predominance and few have survived. In human life and history, as well, few peoples and individuals have been chosen, and many have been left behind. This raises the question of whether the evil—which is extinction—does not emerge out of that very process of choice by which history moves forward.

10 Chosen for creation and seemingly chosen for the longest record of suffering among the peoples of mankind, the Jews pay a terrible price for the special role in human history God has given them.

11   Those who are chosen by God for true creation in cultural life are often those who also choose themselves. Such cultural creators stand in strong contrast to the Hebrew prophets, who almost always are chosen reluctantly, against their will.

12   Just as there are peoples and individuals who are chosen in history for a special place in creation, so there are chosen periods and times.

13   Two measures of the chosenness of cultural creation are the recognition it is given and the place it comes to have in the remembrance, or consciousness, of mankind.

⊠   ⊠   ⊠

4. THE CHOSENNESS OF PEOPLES IN CREATION: SECONDARY CHOSENNESS

1   The direct chosenness that is God's revelation to Israel is built on a historical covenant of mutual obligation that is renewed from generation to generation. The chosenness of other peoples in various fields of creation is not built on such a specific promise.

2   There are periods in history when creative power is centered in a single people. Consider, for example, the ancient Greeks' revelation of philosophy, their creation of a new dramatic literature, their opening the human mind to scientific inquiry. Consider the predominance at various times of the Italians and Dutch in painting, the Germans in music, the Americans in political thought, the Elizabethan English in drama, the nineteenth-century Russians in a new form of spiritual fiction.

3 Works of great creation often appear as miraculous when set against the background of other generations that failed in their striving for true creation. Works of creation often appear as gifts that mysteriously come to a people or individual at a certain time.

4 How do we explain the fact that peoples (i.e., Germans, Russians) who have been exceptionally evil and cruel in history have nonetheless been great in creation? How do we connect their tremendous gifts with tremendous moral failings, and with the idea that God is just and rewards the righteous?

5 Great creation is not only remembered, it is also lived again, generation after generation. The life of works of great creation thus extends beyond and extends the lives of their creators, who in this way seem chosen and blessed as immortal.

6 Why is it that certain peoples have great powers in creation while others have none? Why is it that God does not distribute equally, either among peoples or among individuals, the powers of creation?

7 The disproportionately great Jewish contribution in recent times to fields other than the moral and religious seems also to be a kind of secondary, indirect chosenness. This chosenness seems more the chosenness of the individual and not of the people as people.

8 True creation often has an element of surprise. Thus, peoples who have built their characters in creation in a certain area often do not understand what happens

when out of their repeated efforts comes no new
creation at all.

9   Despite the will to create, often the greatest creation
     comes *unconsciously,* as if it were the result of a tacit
     cooperation between the hidden action of God and
     the inner mind of the creator.

10   It would be possible to make a long list of peoples
     chosen in specific areas of creation, and a much
     longer list of those who worked in those areas without
     creating anything of significance at all.

11   The secondary chosenness of great cultural creators
     involves more willful self-choosing than did the cho-
     senness of Israel by God.

12   The chosenness of peoples in the cultural realm is
     often mistakenly interpreted by them as God's ap-
     proving of their political and military predominance.
     But the sun has set on every human empire known on
     this earth.

13   Cultural history is in one sense nothing other than the
     story of what has been chosen in creation, what is
     higher in human remembrance.

▨   ▨   ▨

5. CHOSENNESS IN CREATION AND HUMAN
REMEMBRANCE

1   The struggle to be chosen in creation in history is the
     struggle to be remembered from generation to gener-
     ation.

2   We assume that those creations we remember after
    hundreds, even thousands, of years — that those cre-
    ations *chosen* by collective human judgment — will be
    those chosen by God for eternity. But where is there
    proof of this? Haven't there been aspects of reality
    that have persisted millions of years, only to then fade
    and die?

3   The Jewish promise that each individual can, through
    his acts of righteousness, contribute to redemption is
    implicitly the promise that each individual may be
    rewarded (chosen for remembrance) in the conscious-
    ness of God.

4   In one important sense, human creation is, in its
    effort to create eternal remembrance, an effort to
    conquer death.

5   The present generation is the ultimate judge of all that
    has happened in human history, until the next gener-
    ation comes.

6   Insecure in its knowledge of the eternal memory of
    God, mankind strives to create, generation to gener-
    ation, a this-worldly collective memory that will en-
    dure into the vaguely distant future.

7   The Jews are commanded time and again by God to
    remember their miraculous deliverance from Egypt.
    This remembrance in a sense constitutes a funda-
    mental act in their creation by God and their creation
    of themselves as a people. Chosenness in creation is in
    this way achieved through remembrance.

8   The greatest works of creation are those each new
    generation can learn from. They are works that must

Eretz Israel

Wisdom comes from
~~work &~~ words &
wonder & worship

To do (create) something
that lasts is humanity's
effort to conquer death.
-Life as Creation p.10

Jesus & Resurrection = Human
Endurance = Conquering Death
ambiguous

be eternally returned to if mankind is to know the highest in itself. *Tanach* is in this sense the central moral and religious creation God has given to mankind.

9   The chosenness of the Jews is given by God in revealing to mankind its mission of redemption. But it is also necessary to try to understand how the creative acts of other peoples also contribute to the overall process of human development and redemption, and how remembrance of these acts is also part of the long process of historical redemption.

10   There must be a remembrance beyond the temporal if the temporal is to endure. Only God in eternity can assure that what appears great in human terms will in fact endure.

11   There is so much creation believed chosen for greatness in its own time and so little that endures in a significant way through time.

12   Can history be seen as a struggle between peoples to decide who will have the power to choose in the end — that is, who will survive and who will remember? Hasn't it been the task of Israel to teach that it is God and God alone who will remember?

13   If there is a competition between generations in creation as to which will be the true consciousness and remembrance of God, there is no clear human means of knowing how God will decide. One idea holds that God already knows and has in mind the whole process, generation by generation, from inside as each one sees it, and all taken together as God alone sees it.

⊠   ⊠   ⊠

6. MORAL AND CULTURAL CREATION AND HISTORICAL REDEMPTION

1 The highest works of secondary creation, the greatest human works of culture, are works in which man serves God ideally by imitating God as creator.

2 The work of creation that God demands of mankind as a whole and of the people of Israel especially is the creation of an ideal society in justice. The creation of such a society seems more connected to the moral life of every man than to the cultural life of the great individual creators.

3 The great works of culture serve God's purpose for humanity by moving it into progressively higher realms of feeling and thought.

4 It is possible to dream of an ideal society in which each and every individual becomes an outstanding creator not only in moral but also in cultural life. But then where would be that process of chosenness that is ordinarily connected with the singling out of works of greatness?

5 By contributing to the overall well-being of mankind, the works of cultural creation—the great works of secondary chosenness—contribute to the process of God's redemption of mankind in history.

6 So many life forms, so many species, so many peoples, so many individuals have appeared only to disappear. It is difficult to understand the redeeming value of so much destruction and extinction in the world's history.

7   As time passes, more and more great cultural works are added to the store of human cultural creation. But this progress does not guarantee that mankind is, in moral and religious terms, any closer to redemption.

8   Ideally, the process of redemption should mean that all mankind is moving toward the recognition of the One Creator, moving toward living by God's moral law.

9   Nowhere is it written that God demands of each and every one of us that he be Shakespeare or Einstein.

10 It is possible to argue that new aesthetic and scientific revelations also elevate mankind morally. Mankind is somehow less, after all, when it does not have within itself that vision of reality that its greatest secular thinkers have given it.

11 The growth in knowledge, in understanding, in power over the external world, and in consciousness of self, which has accelerated since the scientific revolution, has deepened and broadened mankind's conception of reality. And it is possible to suggest that in time this process too (even if it takes generations) will help bring mankind closer to God.

12 The more we know, the closer we come to God, if only in knowledge.

13 Mankind's re-creation of itself through increasing mastery of external nature has not led to a new stage of moral perfection in human history. Instead, paradoxically, the techniques of progress have been used as a means for evils beyond any known in the past.

Clearly, then, scientific and cultural advances are by
no means a guarantee that mankind is moving surely
on the path to moral and religious redemption.

⊠   ⊠   ⊠

7. CREATION AS ONGOING PROCESS OF MANKIND AS A WHOLE

1 Creation is not simply a matter of the work of
outstanding individuals and peoples. It is also an
ongoing process in which small changes are being
introduced all the time by large numbers of largely
anonymous creators.

2 Hasn't mankind moved closer to adopting—at least in
ideal—the moral and religious principles in which the
Jewish people were instructed by God? Is not a
considerable portion of mankind closer today than
ever before to believing in the sacred character of
human life, of individuals having equal rights before
the law? Hasn't mankind today—at least in ideal—
come closer than ever before to adopting the Hebrew
prophetic ideal of a world order built not on the
notion of empire or conquest but on that of universal
peace? And isn't this progress of a kind even if the
realization of the ideal is still remote?

3 The scientific revolution, the communications revolution, the process whereby man has learned to antici-
pate and create inventions—all these processes seem
to prove mankind is greater in technical power than it
ever dreamed. And this process seems to have such a
momentum of its own that it is difficult to understand
what the outcome of it will be.

4   Mankind's creative capacity enables it to usurp more
    and more powers once believed exclusively divine,
    including the power to destroy all life on earth and,
    more remarkably, perhaps to synthesize new forms of
    life in the laboratory.

5   Mankind now seems at the point of being able to
    re-create itself physically as a species and perhaps to
    invent other, more durable, nonorganic intelligent spe-
    cies as replacement for it in exploring the outer regions
    of the universe. But what possible meaning for overall
    human redemption can this kind of process suggest?

6   How is it possible to speak of an overall pattern of
    progress when there have been such vast destructions,
    even in recent generations? And hasn't the greatest
    destruction in the history of God's chosen people
    occurred at a time and in a place when mankind was
    far more advanced than ever before in its knowledge
    of the world?

7   The processes of creation in science and technology
    are competitive in that, through them, various soci-
    eties seek advantage and power over one another.
    This is the major reason for the potential destructive-
    ness of such creative processes.

8   The unintended destructive consequences of scientific
    and technical creation have become more and more
    apparent in time. But this has not halted, and will not
    halt, the process of Invention by which mankind, in
    bettering its situation, further complicates it.

9   Countless individuals and collectives act to forward
    their own conception of advancement and self-interest
    without understanding the consequence of their ac-
    tions on the movement of mankind as a whole. But, if
    all of history is the plan and will of God, then many

of these processes, too, must play their part in the overall story of redemption.

10   In all the creative action of mankind as a whole, there is no sign that present and future generations have discovered the way to revitalize or bring back to life past generations and make them the beneficiaries of the overall forward sweep of history.

11   The ongoing process of historical creation is too vast and indeterminable to be understood in precise terms by this or by any other "present" generation.

12   The vast increase in human skills, powers, and creative capacities (even in the invention of new arts) does not mean there is now some new overall creative center by which mankind as a whole exercises greater control over its own destiny than it did in the past.

13   The more we know, the more we know we do not know: this is as true as ever. Knowledge alone is not enough for understanding, and understanding in the deepest sense requires faith in God's plan for the overall redemption of mankind.

▨   ▨   ▨

8. ULTIMATE LIMITATIONS IN HUMAN CREATIVE POWERS

1   In order to have absolute power and self-sufficiency, mankind must usurp and replace God. But so long as the speed of light is infinite, every new effort at

building the Tower of Babel will be confined to one small interval of the universe.

2 All knowledge of Shakespeare and his times has not enabled mankind to produce his equal, much less his better.

3 If mankind should ever reach the stage where it claimed to be its own creator, it would have to do this by a deliberate act of forgetting. This willful self-deception would be only another piece of evidence proving how far we are, not only from perfection, but also from basic decency and goodness.

4 Great masterpieces and great geniuses come unexpectedly, miraculous occurrences that mankind has not learned to manufacture singly, much less mass produce. The invention of inventions is, even in the most advanced communities in modern times, confined to science and technology and has no real place in arts and humanities.

5 Our inability to overcome human nature is evident in our inability, in worlds of wealth and plenty, to create lives for ourselves that are happy and free of suffering.

6 We can send our instruments farther into the universe than we can ever hope to bodily send ourselves.

7 Our inability to overcome the evil in ourselves and re-create ourselves as wholly good creatures shows yet another way in which we fall short of the transcendent, the divine.

8 Mankind is forever encountering unintended consequences of its own actions and decisions. Complete

control of ourselves and our world is simply not granted to us.

9   There has never been a human genius supreme in all realms of creation, of equal ability in all that he has tried. Every great power in one direction seems to compromise development in another.

10 The most poignant and painful of all human limitations is the inability to help those we love when they are most in need of help.

11 We will never have the power to bring back to life in this world those who have passed from it.

12 The indefinite extension of individual human life (should we achieve this) would deprive us of that sense of time's preciousness that often makes our actions especially meaningful.

13 There are inherent contradictions in the very structure of life and experience. Any humanly achieved perfection is in itself always bound to be imperfect.

▢   ▢   ▢

9. FURTHER LIMITATIONS IN THE CREATION OF MANKIND: THE CREATURE IN THE MIDDLE

1   We are born in the middle of history and will die somewhere further along in the middle.

2   God created all in goodness at the beginning, and God will redeem all in goodness at the end. But the human

struggle is, by and large, in the middle, generation after generation.

3   We live in the middle of history and, throughout our lives, observe the drama unfold. We must leave before we see the most interesting chapters and learn what will happen next to the loved ones we leave behind.

4   It is possible to imagine that God takes us to the higher world, and from there enables us to see the human drama unfold in real time. Or perhaps God endows us with the divine power of seeing it all, beginning to end. But what then of the suspense of living it?

5   To live in the middle of history is to know one has responsibility for only one small part of the whole — a small part upon which, in some way, the outcome of the whole depends.

6   This is the meaning of creating in freedom: we take the responsibility, which is ours to take, even if it is small and limited in time.

7   To understand one's own life as part of a middle generation is to understand that the history of one's own people is larger than one's own life and perception. To take responsibility in the middle is to understand with humility that one is only one small actor, in one scene, in a vast drama that has gone on and will go on for ages.

8   Those who take responsibility for history in their own time contradict the tradition of simply waiting for miraculous deliverance from on high. Instead, if they are people of faith, they prepare for such deliverance.

9   It is possible to pray for the Messiah, to believe in the coming of the Messiah, and yet believe strongly in the necessity of acting in history in one's own time.

10 Too many human generations have known with certainty that all history will climax in their own generation. There have already been too many "ends" in the middle, which have not been the true end.

11 To feel oneself only in the middle and not at the beginning or end of history is to have a certain humility about one's own place in creation.

12 So many generations have come before and so many generations will come after, yet we have only one short time that is our own.

13 There are those who see each generation in the middle as a descent from an ideal beginning. And there are those who see history as a gradual ascent to a greater and greater good from generation to generation. But for those living in the middle of the struggle, the bringing of greater good to the world in their own time might be, in itself, all the duty and justification they need rightfully ask of themselves.

⊠   ⊠   ⊠

10. CREATION AND THE OVERALL DEVELOPMENT OF MANKIND

1   Is mankind progressing toward greater closeness to God, to greater recognition of the God of Israel as the *one* God of the universe? Do we consider the spread

of Christian and Muslim conceptions of the deity as mankind's moving closer to the God of Israel? Are they, too, part of the overall process of redemption?

2   What does the future progress and development of mankind mean to the millions of individuals and thousands of generations forever left behind, if there is no higher world of redemption beyond this one?

3   There is progress in mankind's understanding of the world, a progress that has greatly accelerated in recent centuries. But there is imperfect translation of this progress into the creation of the ideal society in justice, the end to which, the Jewish tradition teaches, history must come.

4   There now seems the likelihood that mankind will begin creating new societies on other planets long before human society has come to perfection. This raises the question of whether mankind will re-create itself in physical and mental form so as to somehow destroy its own essence.

5   Will mankind be to intelligent life in the universe what the Jews have been to mankind — the teacher of the idea that there is one and only one Creator and Ruler of the universe?

6   The vast realm of dust and darkness in the universe, and the vast numbers of creatures who have been born only to die, raise the question of which remnant of creation God intends to preserve forever. Also raised is the question of whether mankind is moving toward the immortalization of some fragment of itself, or its own total oblivion, or a kind of divine redemption beyond all possible rational understanding.

7   Mankind's increasing ability to re-create not only
    the world but also its own conditions of life raises the
    question of whether it will come at some point to
    the ideal of re-creating itself as single, all-controlling
    consciousness. Will it thereby willfully destroy the
    diversity and freedom so essential to human life as we
    know it?

8   If mankind creates a kind of creature superior to it in
    intelligence and endurance, capable of exploring and
    colonizing new worlds, will it then decide to exit
    gracefully from the world? Or will it still know itself
    as the only creature created in the image of God?

9   There are certain basic goals of mankind—an end to
    hunger and poverty, opportunity in education for
    all—that mankind should have the power to realize in
    the generations ahead. There does seem a real hope of
    mankind solving its basic material problems, but there
    is no sign of mankind being able to solve its funda-
    mental spiritual problems without its turning to God.

10 The pattern has been that there is an increase in
    knowledge without an increase in goodness. This
    suggests that the next stage of human history and
    development should be one in which there is concen-
    tration on the moral development of mankind and the
    bringing about of a worldwide society in justice.

11 Is the return of the Jews to the land of Israel a sign
    that mankind has entered a new and higher stage in its
    redemption?

12 One idea of overall human development is that God
    withdraws direct power in time in order to give
    mankind more and more freedom. Man takes greater
    control of creation in time.

13 For those who believe in the providence of God in history, all actions of mankind in freedom are toward further realization of the divine plan. The overall development of mankind is, paradoxically, freely created by mankind in accordance with a plan preconceived by God.

II

Jewish Creation

⊠   ⊠   ⊠

11. THE JEWS AND RELIGIOUS CREATION

1 God chose the Jewish people. They, in accepting this
choice (from Abraham on), chose to be chosen.
Through them a new religious and moral order would
be given to mankind. In this creation, the Jews are
servants of God.

2 The Jews are the people who do the most to bring
mankind to the belief that there is one and only one
Creator of the universe. The Jewish task throughout
history is to help bring all mankind to the understanding that One God who created and rules the
world cares for His creation.

3 God creates a relationship with the Jews through the
making of a covenant. God, the Creator, chooses the
Jews, but the Jews also act in freedom in agreeing to
be God's chosen people. This special relationship
between God and the Jews—the story of Israel in
time—is another of this people's creative contributions to mankind.

4 In agreeing to be chosen, the Jews agree to live by the teachings of God. They agree to submit themselves to greater demands and restrictions than other peoples. They agree to distinguish themselves, to be re-created as a sacred people especially dedicated to service of God.

5 The Jews' sense of their special relationship to God will, at a later phase of their history, also have great creative significance for them—both as a people and as individuals—even when many lose their sense of religious distinctiveness.

6 Jews make a contribution to mankind through the exemplary quality of their action. Time and again the great act of liberation in Jewish history, the bringing of the people out of slavery from Egypt, becomes emblematic of the human struggle for freedom.

7 The Jews' life and history will become, in time, one of their greatest creations. For many, the proof of the saving power of God, the miraculous character of God's action in history, is given primarily through continued Jewish survival, through test and tribulation, the like of which no other people have known.

8 God gives the Jews freedom, the choice between good and evil. Time and time again the Jews choose evil, are punished, and then turn to God in repentance. This action of repentance serves to bring them closer to God than they were before.

9 Jewish action in history is cocreation with God, the realization of the divine plan, the keeping of the promise God has made to Israel. The promise to make the children of Abraham live through the generations has been renewed from generation to generation. The

promise to return the Jews to their own homeland has required from them the longest act of "keeping faith" in human history.

10   In creation, God established a pattern, an order for the world, a way in righteousness. The Jews were chosen to live that pattern, and their freedom in the truest sense is in their decision to live by the teachings God has given them.

11   The Jews are chosen by God to be the transmitters to mankind of fundamental moral principles. And the Jews are commanded to teach not only by word but by deed and example as well.

12   Though the Creator creates free creatures who also can create, there remains always an overwhelming asymmetry in the relationship between God and the Jews, God and mankind. For God has created these "human creators," but they—even in their realization of the divine plan for humanity—do not create God.

13   All of Jewish history is directed and planned by God so that the free actions of the Jews realize this plan whether or not they are aware of it.

⊠   ⊠   ⊠

12. THE JEWS' RE-CREATION OF THEMSELVES IN HISTORY

1   Time and again the Jews must choose between the way of God and the way of idolatry. Time and again their history is created by a fundamental moral choice: whether to walk with, or turn from, God.

2   Time and again the Jews are faced with unexpected challenges and threats. Time and again they must act in uncertainty and pray for the miraculous deliverance of God. They are the people who are always made to feel a desperate need for God.

3   The people chosen to be closest to God through their freedom in creation are those who time and again know the futility of their action when God is not with them. The Jews are taught by their own experience not to trust in the ruling worldly powers of their time but in the Power that is in and beyond all time.

4   The ideal is that God miraculously helps the Jews the moment they show the slightest sense of repentance.

5   The commandment to walk in the ways of God is the commandment for the Jews to show the same kind of love, justice, and mercy that God shows them.

6   A great turning point in Jewish history came when Jews stopped waiting for miraculous messianic deliverance from without and began to believe that only through their own action could they put an end to their suffering in exile. The Jewish belief in their own freedom in action helped give them this freedom.

7   The Jews' inability to end their own exile, their living, in a sense, at the mercy of others for two thousand years, meant that they lost a great deal of their collective, creative capacity, their freedom. Much of this capacity would be restored to them only upon their return to the land of Israel.

8   God makes the most stringent demands of those to whom He is closest. Thus, the Jews have been forced to meet the most difficult tests in order to realize God's plan of redemption for them in history.

9   The story of the Jewish struggle for freedom is also
    the story of many horrendous failures. How many
    times in the course of their long exile did the Jews take
    refuge in the belief in a false messiah who led them
    from great suffering to greater disaster?

10 Jewish loss of freedom in the diaspora led to the
    search for freedom in new areas. A people who had
    ceased to create in space created a greater depth in
    time; a people who had ceased creation in the external
    world deepened its creation in the internal world, the
    world of mind and learning.

11 The great Jewish burst of creative activity in the
    modern world was diligently prepared for — uninten-
    tionally — by generations of talmudic study.

12 All Jewish re-creations of self are centered on an
    identity concept given to them by God. Thus the Jews,
    as chosen people, even today do not re-create them-
    selves out of nothing but out of a sense of realizing a
    potential inherent in themselves.

13 Jewish re-creation is the realization of Jewish destiny.
    It is the people's action in realizing the plan of history,
    the promise given to their ancestors by God.

                   ▧   ▧   ▧

13. THE JEWISH CONCEPTION OF THE
RELATION BETWEEN GENERATIONS

1   Abraham is promised that his name will live through
    the generations that come after him. God creates for

him a new kind of immortality, an immortality given
through the lives of others, his descendants.

2   In the biblical narrative, the story of the people is told
as the story of successive generations in relation to
God. In other words, any individual's creation, no
matter how great, is one part of a long story and not
complete in and of itself.

3   It is the duty of Jewish parents to teach their children
how to live by the Torah. The great moral demand
made on the parents is to educate their children to
walk in the ways God has instructed. In the story of
Jewish continuity is the story of Jewish creativity
from generation to generation.

4   The Jews teach that every generation is to see itself as
if it were brought forth out of Egypt, as if it, too,
were present at the giving of the Torah at Sinai. Thus,
for the Jew, the past is not simply past: the deeds of
God in the past live in the present also and are
re-created anew with each generation learning and
living through and by them.

5   Each generation is a story, an end in itself; yet each
generation cannot be understood without understanding the generations that go before and come
after it.

6   Though each generation stands close to God, certain
generations play special roles in history. There was the
generation that went forth from slavery in Egypt, and
then the generation that entered the promised land; in
our own time there has been a wilderness generation
and a generation that has restored the land of Israel to
the people to whom God promised it.

7   There are many unknown generations in Jewish history who seem to have created nothing of special distinction but who performed the essential task of keeping the tradition alive, transmitting it to the generation that came after.

8   There are chosen generations in creation as there are chosen individual creators.

9   The Jew who has no connection with any past or future generation, who lives in his mind and heart for himself and himself alone, is regarded in the Jewish tradition as not having lived at all.

10   Earlier generations seek their redemption in later ones, and later ones seek their inspiration from earlier ones.

11   The Jews also gave the world a particular concept of historical development in which the life of one extended family through the generations is the story of the chosen people. The story of the Jewish people is the continuing story of the family of the patriarch Jacob, whose struggle with the angel of God won for his posterity the name *Israel*.

12   It is both absurd and natural that past generations of Jews see the redemption of their own suffering in the lives of Jewish generations they will never live to know personally.

13   The Jewish dream of future generations redeeming the sins and failings of past ones inevitably leads present generations to look beyond themselves. The "here and now" is never enough for a people that must redeem all time.

▧   ▧   ▧

14. JEWISH PEOPLE AS PEOPLE OF CREATION

1 Along with the fundamental religious, moral, and literary creation in biblical antiquity, the Jews have made creative contributions to mankind throughout their long history. Perhaps most remarkable are the revolutionary contributions in modern times in many fields of creative work long thought impossible for them.

2 The Jews as a people of creation in antiquity were a people of time more than of space, of the ear more than of the eye, of the literary arts more than of the visual arts, of the moral and religious world rather than of the purely aesthetic. All the individual and collective overcomings of historical character by individual Jews in modern times (and by the people of Israel in the land of Israel) confirm this.

3 For two thousand years, the Jews were accused of having no physical strength, no capacity for working the land or fighting their own battles. Upon their return to Israel in modern times, the Jews seem to have re-created their own character, proving themselves capable of skills long denied them. They thus give mankind an example of the powers of self-re-creation and self-overcoming that others, also accused of being inferior, might use. This is one great achievement of Jewish creation.

4 The sense of being chosen for something special informs the lives of many individual Jewish creators. The collective religious role of the Jews has repeatedly been taken by individuals as referring to their own private work.

5   The great emphasis the Jews placed on learning during the years of exile prepared them well for the modern world in which creative power would be increasingly understood as the power of knowledge. Creation for the Jews in the modern world involved an encounter between minds long used to intellectual work with new modes of knowledge open to further development.

6   Because they did not grow naturally within the world of modern learning, Jews came to many fields with a new way of seeing. They could see from within and without at once and were thus able to make the kinds of new connections that are often the essence of creative endeavor.

7   In modern times, individual Jews have invented whole new fields of human inquiry as if they were not content to be scientists only but had to be lawgivers and prophets as well. Durkheim, Freud, Einstein— each was a modern Moses in his own small world.

8   The tendency to make a religious activity out of their own cultural activity often typifies individual Jewish creators who have abandoned their people's religion.

9   In biblical religious revelation, the Jews are given an understanding that will transform the very meaning of mankind. In modern learning, Jews often work to re-create fields of knowledge as a way of helping themselves belong to mankind.

10 A small people had to create something of supreme value if it were to survive: so, too, individuals who felt themselves weak and small felt they had to make extraordinary contributions to prove their right to survive. Thus, for the Jews, creation often takes the form of a struggle for compensation and survival.

11 The chosenness of the Jews in the world of modern
      creation, their disproportionate contribution to the
      overall cultural and scientific progress of mankind,
      can be seen as a kind of secondary chosenness, a nat-
      ural chosenness. And yet there is a sense that this, too,
      must have some specific religious meaning the indi-
      vidual creators themselves are not aware of at the time.

12 The outburst of individual Jewish creativity in the
      modern era — after a long period of seeming exclusion
      from the general culture — has a miraculous quality. It
      appears as if it is another of God's great and unique
      gifts to the Jewish people.

13 In the modern world, the individual achievements of
      Jews in creation often occur outside the land of Israel,
      but the great collective re-creation is the building of a
      Jewish society within the promised land.

                    ▨   ▨   ▨

15. CERTAIN CHARACTERISTICS OF JEWISH CREATION AND CREATORS

1   For the Jew, commentary on religious texts is a
      principal form of creation. This "learning" is a kind of
      perpetual re-creation of traditional sources. For the
      religious Jew, this kind of creation is higher than any
      other as it involves direct connection with God's holy
      words of Torah. The practical aim or result of this
      learning is not important. The "learning" itself is
      understood as service of God in the highest sense.

2   In a small land, layers of meaning are built through
      returning time and again to the same place. So too in
      exile the Jews, small and crowded in space, find the

true area for mental exploration and development in worlds of time more than in worlds of space.

3   Inside and outside their own tradition of mind and the tradition of the West, the Jews, in their search for enlightenment, time and again find new ways of recombining and seeing reality. Their in-betweenness helps them reshape the existing categories into new fields of their own.

4   The Jewish habit of relying on the inner mind leads to a new way of making art of abstraction.

5   The prophetic element works in many Jewish minds, even when they feel themselves having lost connection to a personal God. Many modern Jewish intellectual workers believe themselves chosen to reveal the ultimate truth of reality, the special revelation hidden in history and nature's impersonal laws.

6   Because the Jews in the diaspora did not know their place, they rushed anywhere they could to make a place. This included entering fields of creation in which considerable numbers of Jews had never worked before.

7   To prove they are as good as the Gentiles, the Jews must always try to be better. Thus, the Jews have much in common with other minorities who desperately need to belong. But in the Jews' case, the ambition is made more intense by their own displaced sense of religious chosenness.

8   The same law applies for the Jews as for other peoples, and most of their effort at creation leads to mediocre results.

9   The revolutionary impulse in much modern Jewish creative activity comes in part from their sense of

never really being able to belong to worlds—even in
learning—they had long been outside of.

10   In modern literature, the Jew becomes the central figure of the culture as a whole in the work of both Jew
(Kafka) and non-Jew (Joyce), but only when that central figure is estranged from the culture he is a part of.

11   Even when the Jews make aesthetic values their
principal ones they do it with a moral and religious
intensity that testifies to their fundamentally moral-
religious character.

12   Self-denial and self-hatred also play a part in Jewish
creation in the modern world. This is perhaps most
clearly illustrated in the great part the Jews played in
the creation of an international movement, commu-
nism, in which the Jews hoped to be assimilated. This
movement they repudiated and persecuted them, not
as citizens of mankind but as Jews.

13   Jewish daring in creation often seems to come out of
a desperate sense that the Jews have nothing further
to lose. Jewish greatness in creation often comes
against all odds and improbabilities: it comes as a
kind of miracle, the like of which the Jewish people
have known in rescue and redemption time and time
again in their history.

⊠   ⊠   ⊠

16. JEWISH CREATION: INTERACTION WITH AND LEARNING FROM OTHER PEOPLES

1   Time and again the Jews meet peoples more advanced
than them from whom they learn. This learning (e.g.,

from medieval Spain and modern Europe) has contributed greatly to Jewish powers of creation.

2   Jewish history can be read as a long list of meetings with successive civilizations, each of which has contributed to Jewish development. And yet, what is essential to Jewish creation was learned not in meeting with other peoples but in meeting with God.

3   Peoples more materially advanced than the Jews were involved in pagan idol worship and human sacrifice. In the moral and religious realm, then, the Jews usually had to strive *not* to learn from their more advanced neighbors.

4   The turning from the modern world, the refusal to learn anything outside the commentary on their own religious writings, left many Jewish communities defenseless in the modern world. Learning from others can also be a form of self-defense, if used wisely.

5   Learning from others requires a certain humility. But many Jews in their self-effacing fawning before the supposedly superior culture of the French, the Germans, the English, the Russians, and nowadays the Americans revealed only their spiritual poverty and ignorance of their own heritage.

6   Jews in the modern world learn less from a people than from a tradition of inquiry that uses methods Jewish traditional learning does not. Such methods (e.g., scientific, experimental) are not the possession of any people but of mankind as a whole.

7   For 2,000 years, the chosen people of history did not make a critical scientific study of their own history. Only in the late eighteenth century did individual Jews

begin discovering new methods for broadening their understanding of their own people's past.

8   There is a kind of mistaken apologetic view of Jewish creativity that supposes Jews have always understood and known more than others in every field of inquiry. This kind of narrow conception of total human creativity works to limit the Jewish appreciation of the way God has interacted with the whole of humanity.

9   The meeting with modern scientific and historical methods not only enabled the Jews to make great contributions to mankind as a whole but also was instrumental in their re-creation as a people. It helped provide means of action for realizing the centuries-long dream of return to the land of Israel.

10 There are by this time signs of a new maturity among religious Jews in being confronted with cultures and ways of thought outside the Jewish tradition. Many areas of mind once off-limits are now being worked in by religious Jews.

11 In learning from others, Jews often prepare themselves for a new stage of their own cultural re-creation.

12 Choosing what to learn and what to deplore in the teaching of others is another way of exercising freedom, choosing between good and evil, and creating.

13 If there are intelligent life forms in other worlds, will we also be able to learn from them in wisdom and humility?

⬚   ⬚   ⬚

17. JEWISH CREATION AND HATRED OF THE JEWS

1 God chose the Jews even though He knew this would make them the most hated people in the history of mankind. No people wants to know that it is less valued, less loved, than another.

2 Jewish physical weakness, combined with spiritual greatness and later intellectual distinction, created the conditions by which evil hatred could lead to repeated efforts at the Jews' physical destruction.

3 The hatred and resentment the Jews experienced from other peoples helped them to create mechanisms of survival and adaptability that frequently worked. But there was no way to use these devices to escape from the systematic destruction devised for them by the European people, which prided itself on being supreme in all things — and was surely supreme in one — the doing of evil.

4 Christianity and Islam each has its own separate tradition of repaying with evil those who provided them with their first understanding of God.

5 The price the Jews have had to pay for being loved so strongly by God has been being hated so strongly by humanity.

6 It is natural to resent those who are more successful than us, those who do better than us. But the wish to destroy them comes only when we sense they are depriving us of our own world. Thus, the closer the Jews came to being at the center of creation in various European societies, the more strongly they were hated.

7   The Christian son accuses the Jewish father of having
    tried to murder him so he can justify his own desire to
    be rid of the father's conscience.

8   Not only do other peoples envy the Jews, the Jews
    also envy other peoples. This has played a part in
    Jewish creation, in the Jewish learning to take upon
    themselves the character of other peoples. Time and
    again the Jews have known how to imitate and
    become the others in the effort to belong to worlds
    they eventually discovered were not their own.

9   Most peoples consider themselves chosen at some
    point of their history. How difficult it must be for a
    people to relate to a prior claim of chosenness,
    especially one based not on position or power in the
    world but on closeness to God.

10 The Christians envied the Jews for what no people in
    antiquity would have thought to envy: their suffering.

11 Envy of the Jews appears to be a constant theme of
    human history that will not disappear until the mes-
    sianic age when all know God is One.

12 The projection of one's own forbidden impulses upon
    the scapegoat is the simple psychological device of
    much hatred of the Jews. The Jews are frequently
    accused of everything the others inwardly know is
    wrong with themselves.

13 The effect of others' hatred of the Jews is also
    expressed in desperate efforts on the part of Jews to
    re-create themselves as others. In other words, hatred
    of the Jews also leads to that cowardly kind of Jewish
    response known as assimilation, the sacrifice of one's

true self for a promised self that will never be completely real.

⊠   ⊠   ⊠

18. JEWISH CREATION AND THE ONGOING STRUGGLE FOR SURVIVAL

1 God's promise to Abraham, the covenant renewed from generation to generation, means for Jews of faith that the people of Israel can never die.

2 The Jewish work of literary creation that has meant most to mankind, *Tanach,* the Bible, promises that so long as mankind knows itself and its own spiritual history, it will keep alive the memory of the Jews.

3 Only by tracing generation to generation the persecutions of the Jews can one fully understand the miracle of Jewish survival. Only by understanding the courage and risk required in being true to their tradition can one understand the greatness of the Jewish history of survival.

4 In one sense, what has kept the Jews most alive is their own tradition of learning, of *Gemara* study. This vast tradition of commentary, this great network of meanings, is by and large known only by the Jews themselves and has been a primary source of their internal strength.

5 The strength of the Jewish family has been a central element in Jewish survival through the centuries. The Jews had clear rules as to how to preserve and develop the family—the laws given by the Torah.

6   A fair account of Jewish survival should also include the story of the failed turnings, the mistakes, and the destructions that might have been avoided.

7   The defense of hiding in our own world, which worked at one time in our history, could not work when the totalitarian enemy used the most modern means of communication and transport to reach us in remote places. At a certain point, escaping from reality no longer proved an adequate defense against it.

8   The building of an army and state of our own is in part the Jewish people's response to our own historical helplessness, our own inability to prevent the destruction of one-third of our own people. The creation of this means of self-defense has provided a new means not only for ensuring Jewish survival but also for enhancing Jewish dignity.

9   The diaspora devices of bargaining and bribing, of courting the favor of this petty tyrant or that, helped the Jews remain alive in exile. In order to survive, it was often necessary to bend and bow and suffer quiet humiliation while waiting and praying for the eventual time of redemption.

10 Waiting for the Messiah and praying to God did not save countless religious Jews from destruction in Nazi Europe. In some cases, God helped those who tried to help themselves.

11 There is a continual temptation in Jewish history for individuals to abandon their collective identity in order to ensure their own personal survival. These individual losses to assimilation have no doubt had their effect on the overall strength of the people.

12   The traits that saved many individual Jews from destruction — courage, ingenuity, decisiveness, quickness of mind, ability to scorn convention and invent remarkably — have also characterized the state of Israel in confronting a vast host of larger and more powerful enemies.

13   God gave to the prophets of Israel the plan for securing Jewish survival: the creating of a world of justice and peace in which all will flow to the mountain of the Lord in Jerusalem.

⌧   ⌧   ⌧

19. CREATION AND THE STATE OF ISRAEL

1   The Jewish return to Israel was an effort to reassume responsibility in history, an effort to re-create the Jewish people as free in deciding its own destiny.

2   The miraculous quality of the Jewish creation in returning to build the Jewish state is made most apparent when it is understood as fulfillment of a divine promise. After 2,000 years of suffering and keeping this promise alive, the Jewish people acted to help realize it.

3   The perfect example of divine and human cooperation is the Jewish return to the land of Israel. God planned and promised the return, and the Jewish people acted upon this promise and began to fulfill it.

4   In creating the state of Israel, the Jews revived a language long thought dead in everyday life. They also re-created their own character by doing the kinds of

work others had believed them incapable of doing.
They came to excel as farmers and soldiers, precisely
the areas in which they were thought totally incapable.

5   The return of the Jews to the land of Israel meant that
once again there was a collective center of creation. It
meant the end to a kind of powerlessness and helplessness before others that had in one sense made their
history a story of disaster after disaster.

6   The re-creation of Jewish communal life in Israel was
attained only after the dedicated effort and sacrifice
of a large number of individuals who put the collective goal before the private individual goal of achievement in creation.

7   Upon their return to Israel, instead of finding themselves in the situation where an ideal, just society
would be readily built, the Jews found themselves in a
bitter national struggle against many enemies. The
return, in itself, did not immediately bring about a
messianic perfection. Instead, it required a long
struggle that, in turn, brought forth and tested new
creative powers in the Jews.

8   The Jewish dream has been to realize the biblical
promise and create a society that would be a light to
the Gentiles. In reviving the language of Hebrew for
use in daily life, in struggling courageously against
more numerous enemies, in building a new society on
foundations of an ancient culture, the Jews of Israel
have set this example—and this when at times the
society seems in danger of succumbing to an easier
ideal or success and becoming just another Western
democratic consumer society.

9   The ongoing struggle to re-create Israel as an ideal
society and holy nation continues. But the very exist-

ence of the state of Israel, however imperfect the state is, is proof of a miraculous, redemptive power in history.

10 Israel contains within itself the possibility of uniting two kinds of creation, two kinds of creative ideal: first, in being the holy nation that serves God and helps lead the world to worship of the One God, and second, in being master in all fields of secondary creation and making outstanding achievements in world culture.

11 The rules of chosenness, which apply to all peoples in creation, mean that the Jews in Israel are limited to excelling in certain well-defined areas. There are other areas of creation that require levels of resources Israel simply does not have.

12 The Jew who creates for mankind while in Israel also helps realize his own people's historical goal — the creative ideal of combining two kinds of creation at once.

13 Israel itself is an ongoing creation that must struggle to become the society God promised the Jews, a model and center of religious understanding for all humanity.

᙭   ᙭   ᙭

20. JEWISH CREATION AND HUMAN REDEMPTION

1 The Jews were chosen by God to help bring mankind to recognition of the One Creator, God and to provide for mankind a new, higher code of morality by which it could become fully human.

2   The final redemption in human history is connected
     with the Jews' returning to the promised land and
     establishing there a new kind of just society. Just as
     there can be no justice and peace for Israel without
     there being justice and peace for mankind as a whole,
     so the justice and peace of humanity is dependent on
     that of Israel.

3   In the divine drama of human redemption, which is
     history in creation, every people has its role. But the
     role of the Jews is central as it involves helping to instill
     the vision of God that will unite humanity in goodness.

4   The collective role of the Jews in the story of human
     redemption is seemingly contradicted by the sinful
     actions of individual Jews. But these contradictions,
     and the opportunities they present for repentance,
     may also be seen as part of the overall process of
     human redemption.

5   But how does the Jewish believer rationally explain
     the fact that monotheism has become the faith of a
     considerable portion of mankind through the work of
     two faiths that rejected Judaism, that persecuted Jews
     for generations? What is the lesson of history we are
     meant to learn by this?

*Christianity
Islam*

6   How is it possible to believe that what happens in one
     final generation or series of generations will redeem
     all that has gone before?

7   As the Jewish return to the land of Israel has not
     brought about a complete perfection—a messianic
     end—but rather a long process of striving toward that
     end, it is to be expected that the process of redemption
     will not end in our own time but will continue for
     many, many generations.

8 The process of redemption is, in one sense, nothing other than the whole process of history itself; both the early and later generations participate in it. There is also the promise of a redemption beyond this process, one beyond time, which God will make miraculously for us all.

9 The present generation is the end to which all previous history has striven and, at the same time, is only a stage on the way to future generations. Each generation must demand of itself to make its contribution to the whole process of redemption.

10 The struggle for redemption is a striving for sanctity. The Jews are required to live by the teachings of God so as to attain a higher level of morality that sets them apart from others and makes them an example to follow.

11 The striving for redemption is also the striving for overall human well-being, including material well-being. In this sense, the scientific and technological achievements of mankind also contribute to the process of religious redemption.

12 It might be claimed that, in antiquity, it was Jewish collective religious creation that most influenced mankind, while in modernity, it has been the creation of individual Jews that has most accelerated the process of human redemption.

13 Is it possible that the Jewish contribution to human redemption will continue in a time when civilization has extended into space and that, in these other worlds, too, there will be a movement to realize the plan of the universe given by God?

III

God and Creation

⊠   ⊠   ⊠

21. GOD'S JUSTICE AND THE WORLD-TO-COME

1 The suffering and injustices of this world would make the concept of a just God inconceivable were it not possible to imagine the compensation God will provide in the world-to-come.

2 In twentieth-century Europe, more than one million Jewish children were cruelly deprived of their lives before they could live them. It is impossible to believe in justice without somehow also believing that they will have their own real lives in the world-to-come.

3 It is possible to argue that the suffering of a year, a day, even an instant (if the sufferer bears no responsibility for it) can never be justly compensated. Eternities upon eternities of bliss cannot erase the experience of one mother whose child was forcibly taken from her, or of one child who saw his father beaten to a humiliating death.

4 As real achievements in life usually involve effort and pain, so the new lives given in compensation must, in the world-to-come, also involve effort and pain. Such effort and pain will be for a purpose, then, and will enhance human dignity rather than destroy it.

5 As the injustice human beings often suffer on earth is beyond our comprehension, we in faith must suppose that the blessing they will receive in the world-to-come is also beyond our understanding.

6 Just as the good must be compensated in the world-to-come for the evils they have suffered in this world, so the evil must be punished for the crimes they have escaped judgment for in this world.

7 Out of love for the innocent who have suffered unjustly, we desperately pray for God's other world.

8 The fundamental Jewish idea of God's rewarding good for good and evil for evil makes logical and religiously correct the prayer that God do justice in the world-to-come for those who have suffered unjustly on earth.

9 If God makes accountings of justice only for communities and peoples and not for individuals, then our individual lives lose a fundamental dimension of their meaning.

10 It may be absurd to believe that God will give new life in other worlds to those who have unjustly lost their lives in this one. But this is what the rules of justice, given by God, demand.

11 It is not only souls that have been lost but life stories as well. Just compensation for the innocents murdered before they could truly live on earth must mean more than restoration of their souls; it must mean opportunity for making new lives in other worlds.

(12) For those whose heart and soul was in studying Torah
in this world and who were deprived of this suddenly
and prematurely, a new world would mean an eternity
of Torah study. But what of those who had other
kinds of life activity, other kinds of creation, as their
service to God? Will God make the other world for
them as interesting and diverse a place as the earth
was before it was taken from them?

13   We must believe that God has blessings prepared for
us in the world-to-come that we have not known the
like of in this one. These blessings are given in
proportion to the degree the person has suffered
unjustly in this world.

▩   ▩   ▩

22. THE NEED FOR GOD

1   The most powerful proof for the existence of God is
the human understanding that without God we would
be unable to save those we love.

2   Anyone who wishes for the eternal life of what he
loves needs God.

3   We need God because we understand how great are
our own limitations, even in helping ourselves.

4   The need for God is strong in those who would have
a complete understanding of the world and who have
understood they cannot attain this themselves. Only
God may have that kind of total understanding many

of us have worked lifetimes to attain and know we will never have.

5   If there is no God, then injustice and evil in this world will triumph eternally.

6   There are those who especially need God at their greatest moments of happiness and blessing. There are those who need One to be grateful to.

7   There are only two alternatives: either there is no ultimate purpose to existence, or there is God.

8   Without God, life has no ultimate meaning. The need for God is the need to find reason and purpose for human existence.

9   There are moments in youth, moments in the age of strength, when we are so confident of ourselves that God is, for us, a superfluous hypothesis. But it is doubtful that the largest share of individuals remain fools throughout their lives.

10   Our need for God is so great that we often find ourselves trying to ignore or justify sufferings in the world that we believe a just God would never allow.

11   Those whose deepest need is to understand the world need God when they learn that there is a kind of understanding that is completely beyond human power and possibility.

12   The balancing of reasons, the suspension of judgment in proving the existence of God, is a luxury most of us cannot afford when the whole of our inner being calls for help. It is not that our intellectual integrity must be sacrificed to our need for God but rather that only

God can provide the answers our hearts and our minds most desperately need.

13 So long as there is death, mankind will need God. The deepest human need for life cannot be satisfied by humanity alone. Without God, human nature cannot bring itself to realization and fulfillment.

⊠   ⊠   ⊠

23. GOD'S PROVIDENCE

1 God has a plan for each of us that is revealed in the course of our lives.

2 Our purpose in life is to discover God's plan for us and to help realize it.

3 God sustains the world at all times, but there are certain times when He intervenes especially to help us. God also makes miracles for individuals.

4 If one truly has faith in God's providence, then every evil suffered will be understood as a step toward a greater blessing, even though there are certain evils that seem so great as to make this impossible.

5 There are degrees of God's supervision and intervention in ongoing reality. Those God has chosen, those God is closest to, feel His intervention in a stronger way than do most others.

6 One way of sensing God's providence is through knowing long preparation, rejection, and delay before being miraculously given what one has dreamed

of and striven for all along. We then feel God's providence strongly in the blessings of our lives.

7   We often sense God's providence in the timing of our lives, in help given just as we are about to despair, and in miraculous meetings that come just as we need them.

8   It is impossible for human beings to imagine the way God directs billions of lives, inconceivably large numbers of events and experiences, into a kind of overall order. If the human being builds a model of the mind of God that is merely a magnified version of human reason, the human will have difficulty understanding how there can be providence in the universe.

9   God's providence is His caring for us, His loving us individually.

10   Many of us repeatedly misread God's plan for us, imagining an outcome or path of development that we believe has been promised to us but has not been realized. The way we deal with our disappointments and disillusionments is also part of God's plan for us.

11   God's providence does not mean, as many of us would like to think, that we are chosen by God for happiness only. How many of those especially close to God, from Akiba to Harav Kook, have endured some terrible test at the end of their lives through which they might prove their great devotion to God?

12   God's providence does not work in contradiction to human freedom but is essential to its development. God watches and helps as human beings strive in freedom to realize the plan of their lives, much as a loving parent who worries for his children but under-

stands that, at a certain point in life, it is necessary to let the child go, to make his own way in the world. So does God worry, wait, and watch for the opportunity to provide special help.

13 Those lives that are cut short before they can be lived fully suggest that God's providence does not confine itself to this world but extends to the world-to-come.

⊠   ⊠   ⊠

24. CREATION AND OBEDIENCE TO GOD

1 In Jewish history there is repeated disobedience, and the higher act of creative redemption comes in response to it. This suggests that the disobedience is part of a deeper process through which the divine drama is worked out in time.

2 The great creators in human history are often seen as those who rebel against the conventional wisdom of their time. There have been stages in history when rebellion has been understood as liberation from the teachings of God. This suggests that there is one reading of history that mankind makes from its own limited perspective in the present and a deeper meaning, which only God knows, before, during, and after.

3 Human creation in obedience to God is not the simple, external following of a rule. It is the realization of the deepest inner need and demand of human nature. It is the cry of the soul in the meeting of the revelation of God. It is walking in the way God has commanded us because this is the only possible way we can be at peace with our souls and ourselves.

4   The day-by-day obedience to God in prayer and study, in living by the Torah, is a kind of creation, a sanctification of the life God has given us.

5   Obedience to God as described in the Psalms of David is not passive, lifeless acquiescence but rather a deep, tormented questioning. It is the soul thirsting for God.

6   Why is it that the deepest expressions of freedom in creation often come as acts of worship and obedience to God?

7   Obedience to God may be understood as the deepest of all needs of human nature to earn the love and approval of the Father of us all.

8   One kind of obedience comes out of rational calculation based on fear of punishment; another is formed out of a deep recognition of God's goodness. This recognition and obedience in love is what all humans must strive for.

9   There are those of us who willfully disobey God, calculating that we will be rewarded later on for our repentance. But no one can know for certain how God will ultimately judge — for good or for evil.

10 If children who are good obey their parents out of a desire to also make the parents happy, shouldn't we, too, strive to obey God out of the belief that this is what will give God pleasure?

11 There is a kind of disobedience to God that is borne of love of fellow human beings and dismay at the

apparent injustice of their suffering. It is almost as if there is the human effort to anger God, to provoke some reaction or response. Waiting and hoping for the response is also a kind of recognition of and obedience to God.

12   Job continues to walk in God's ways and continues to obey Him, no matter how clear it is to him that he is suffering unjustly. This kind of obedience is proof of faith in God's ultimate justice.

13   The faith of Israel, the obedience to God through all the years of exile, will eventually be rewarded in restoring the people to the land of Israel. The goodness, which is obedience to God, will also be rewarded by God in time.

▩   ▩   ▩

25. CONSCIOUSNESS AND CREATION

1   Clearly, the ultimate test of any creation is the place it will have in the consciousness of God. What God chooses to remember will live.

2   The great work in creation is, in human terms, that which lives, generation after generation, in the consciousness of mankind. But the number of such past creations is so small in comparison to what is promised to come that it is difficult to know with certainty what will live and what will not.

3   The struggle of the creator for recognition of his work
    is a struggle for a place in the consciousness of
    mankind.

4   It is possible to argue that the overall development of
    human history is such that the collective conscious-
    ness of later generations is more varied and complex
    than earlier ones. But there is no way to know how
    and where this process will end and how God will
    decide which generations' complex consciousness to
    keep alive forever.

5   In creation, as in life, there is a process of chosenness
    that inevitably means the great majority of actions
    and things, lives and works, pass into oblivion. The
    consciousness of mankind cannot possibly preserve
    the greatest part of human creation, and we cannot
    know how the mind of God works to keep alive what
    will be kept alive.

6   We also do not know the hidden recesses of God's
    memory and what may live in divine consciousness
    though seemingly lost to human thought forever.

7   The consciousness of mankind is divided into many
    different communities of remembrance, each strug-
    gling for predominance. It is possible to surmise that
    this competition is decided in the mind of God — and
    this when Israel has not been promised by God so
    much a continual life in mind as an eternal life on
    earth.

8   Israel's service to mankind is to help re-create human
    consciousness so as to be in constant service to God.

9   There is asymmetry between the consciousness of the
    Creator and that of the creation. Our consciousness

must, in fear and love, worship God, while God's must, in some sense, forever be a mystery to us.

10 The Creator demands our recognition, even though we cannot fully hope to understand whom we recognize. The Creator demands our worship, service, and obedience, even when we cannot be fully conscious of whom we worship.

11 The consciousness of mankind makes a creative work live through reinterpreting it, extending its meaning generation to generation. A work, in time, becomes the sum of all the successive readings of it, a product of the collective consciousness of mankind through generations.

12 We cannot understand the precise way in which God is continually reinterpreting and re-creating all creation. And we cannot know how this process, in time, relates to the consciousness of God, which is beyond time.

13 We think of ourselves as real in the world, but we cannot know how real we are and how real we will be in the mind of God.

        ▪   ▪   ▪

26. THE MIND OF GOD

1 The mind of God would have to be beyond our conception (not only physically but logically) if it were to be all powerful. But this is no conclusive reason for not believing it real, for we know how often reality

turns out to be beyond anything we have previously conceived.

2   We desire to know the mind of God because we wish to know if God approves of what we do. But the mind of God, in this sense, is known to us, for we have been given God's teaching as to what is good and what is evil. The Torah expresses the mind of God.

3   In thinking of our relation to the mind of God, we are again and again led into contradiction and impossibility. How can we be free while God controls all? How can we create when all creation is God's possession? How can we worship God as perfectly good when we know God is Creator of good and evil? In pondering questions we cannot answer, we are left with a strong sense of how limited our own minds are and how incomprehensible the mind of God is to us.

4   We do understand the mind of God in certain ways, for instance, when we see what is good in creation. When we know God's blessings in this world, we do know something of the mind of God.

5   Our confusion is not that we do not wholly understand the mind of God but that we understand and do not understand—that our comprehension is partial and contradictory.

6   We see evils in the world that lead us to wonder if the mind of God has not been evil from youth. There are times, then, when we contradict what we know we should believe—that God's mind is wholly good. But whether God will punish us for this, we do not know.

7   The mind of God is reflected within the workings of impersonal nature. This raises the question of whether

there are levels not only of our own comprehension of God but also within the mind of God. But how can we understand this, when God is the One and Only One?

8 The Jewish emphasis on God's transcendence leads many of us to feel that, even when we make clear inferences about the mind of God from solid facts of reality, we are only guessing. It leads us to feel that the mind of God, so long as we know only what we know on earth, will always be a mystery to us.

9 One dream of our higher life in the world-to-come is that there we will be closer to the mind of God than we are now.

10 But if the mind is one aspect only of complex human personality, so it must be one aspect only of the Being of God. Even if we were to know the mind of God, we would not know God.

11 The strong desire to know the mind of God in our everyday life is often the desire to know which decision to make. It can be the expression of our desire to escape our own freedom, or it can be the expression of our desire to realize our freedom in the most righteous way.

12 There is such a great gap between our conception of what mankind—individually and collectively—is capable of knowing and what an all-knowing Creator must know that we sense it absurd to even begin to think about God's omnipotence. This sense of unreality is another test of faith our reason makes for us.

13 The mind of God is fundamentally good and continues to work to redeem mankind. God is the kind Parent who will always have understanding and mercy

for us. We may not know the mind of God completely, but we nonetheless are commanded to trust it
with all our heart.

⊠   ⊠   ⊠

27. THE MIND OF GOD: A COMPARISON OF DIVINE AND HUMAN METHODS OF CREATION

1   God is the only One who can create something out of
    nothing. Yet, every true creation brings to the world
    something that has never been before.

2   Creation is inherent in nature; the higher the creature,
    the more capable it is of creation. Man is the most
    perfect of all God's creatures in that he is capable of
    rich and varied creations. But all of this is small in
    comparison to the worlds of space and time, the great
    distances and dimensions, the whole of everything,
    that God has brought into being.

3   Humans create within the limited space of their own
    lifetimes, while God is within and without all lifetimes
    at once.

4   Each great cultural creator makes a world of his own.
    But this world is also God's — one of the immense
    number of worlds God possesses.

5   Our creation is, ideally, an imitation of the divine
    creation for good. But God's creation is not an
    imitation of ours, since we are God's, and all we make
    is God's.

6   If the mind of God contains all human imaginations
    and the imaginations of all creatures of all other
    worlds, how can any human being possibly hope to
    begin to represent it?

7   We make great efforts at creation, yet we know that
    only a small part of what we do (if anything at all) will
    be remembered. Too often God's creation seems to us
    to be, by and large, a waste, a vast production of
    things of which few are remembered and preserved.

8   If all natural processes are part of God's creation,
    then what we are doing in our scientific investigations
    is searching the mind of God. Any method invented to
    open up new worlds of discovery is also God's.

9   The process of ever more complex realities emerging
    from simpler ones, of higher and higher intelligences
    evolving in time, may be one way the mind of God
    works. But our problem is that, however we in the last
    200 years have expanded our vista of time, we are still
    inside the process. We cannot hope to see all, from
    before and after, as God must.

10 God is the Creator of Good as it is Good and Evil as
    it is Evil. Yet God is wholly good and not evil, and we
    who know the evil within ourselves, even as we strive
    to make it into good, do not understand this.

11 The human being is continually creating and forget-
    ting. We do not know how God remembers but only
    that remembrance of God's commandments is essen-
    tial to our living the true life.

12 We are continually making analogies, projecting our
    own higher capacities onto God. Yet we understand
    that there is no analogy and that the mind of God is
    beyond anything we can humanly imagine.

13 We also seek to read the story of God's creation of the
world in *Bereshit* as a paradigm for all subsequent
human creation. But the methods of mankind, which
are developed in time, prove more varied than what is
given in the initial model. Just as we cannot understand the creations of God by analogy with the
creations of mankind, so we cannot foresee the
varieties of human creation simply by patterning them
after the creation by God.

⌗   ⌗   ⌗

28. CREATING GREATER GOODNESS

1 In the biblical conception the world is empty at the
beginning, and goodness is in filling it with life
through time.

2 God commands, "Be fruitful and multiply." The
creation of new life is understood as a fundamental
good, and this remains true in the Jewish tradition
throughout our long history.

3 If more life is good, then why does God let sin bring
death to the world? Why is the creature made in the
eternal God's image a mortal?

4 The history of mankind over the generations is one of
increasing human power and freedom. Greater goodness is connected with mankind's increasing knowledge, understanding, and power of responsibility over
creation. The paradox is that with this increased
power for creation comes an increased power of

destruction; with increased power for good comes increased power for evil.

5   Increasing power over nature in and of itself is not necessarily good and can lead to evil. The true revolution in history toward greater goodness comes with Abraham's meeting with God and with mankind's assuming a new measure of devotion and faith to the Creator. This process is given its supreme expression in God's meeting with Moses on the mountain, the revelation of the Torah to Israel. This moment of goodness cannot be gone beyond but must be lived again and again in the life and consciousness of each individual Jew.

6   There is an idea of God's plan of creation that maintains that God, in time, successively withdraws from the world so that mankind can have greater opportunity in freedom. This idea is most often used not to explain why the world has become so much better in time but why there are such horrible evils and injustices.

7   There are all kinds of measures by which we might show how a portion of mankind is currently better off than it was generations ago — higher standards of living, longer life spans, more opportunities for work and recreation, better health in old age. These improvements in the human condition attest to the idea that God intends mankind to make overall progress in time.

8   No matter how great the improvement, the truth is that the lifetime of an individual is an incredibly short span of time compared with that of cosmic creation.

9   But can it be supposed that God wants all previous generations to go through what they go through

simply to arrive at greater goodness in the end? Must not there be a way of understanding the world in which goodness is absolute in each individual life?

10 Is there any proof that the individual lives of our generation are equal in goodness to those of the sages, the prophets, and the patriarchs?

11 Mankind's effort at greater goodness in history is like the individual's effort in *Kedushah* to come closer to God. The aim is to slowly move higher, and nearer to God, while understanding that one can never become one with God.

12 While mankind perfects this world in goodness, individuals go on dying.

13 No later generation will create a greater work of goodness than the *Tanach,* nor will any later generation have a greater revelation than that given at Sinai.

❊   ❊   ❊

29. GOD AND THE MYSTERIES OF CREATION

1 Just as we can never completely understand God's nature, so we can never completely understand our own relationship with God.

2 We try to understand the mystery of God's nature by listing all the powers we have and those we would like to have and then attributing these powers to God. But we understand that this is a futile exercise, a childlike

effort to understand a complexity we cannot begin to imagine.

3   We have no idea whether there are other universes beyond those our telescopes can probe. We cannot know how many dimensions and infinitudes there are in the mind of God.

4   Our essential inability to apprehend God, our feeling of the mysterious character of the Creator, helps produce that religious humility, that awe before God that is one aspect of virtue in humanity.

5   We cannot begin to understand how God can at once be concerned with so many different individuals, peoples, communities, and worlds. Even the love of God is a mystery to us.

6   Our inability to understand God completely, our inability to reduce Him to our own level—to control Him for our own purpose, to replace Him with our own human will and demands—is a permanent element of the human condition, a fundamental truth of what we essentially are.

7   Our own sense of wonder and mystery at creation may leave us with a feeling of being wholly estranged from God or may bring us closer to God.

8   We try to understand God's relation to the world by paralleling it to our own relation to the world. But this proves futile when we come to the point of understanding how we are confined within our own world and how God is beyond this and all other worlds.

9   The question of how God created a world that is outside God, how God is one but not one with creation, how God is all and yet all is not God, cannot

be answered by the logic of the human mind. And all the efforts at explanation, whether in philosophy or myth, only augment the sense of our ultimate inability to comprehend God.

10 Why God needs these creatures of dust in worship, why He cares for the service of humanity, is also a mystery that has no real explanation.

11 Those who worship God, those who need and love God, always find proof of God's presence in the miraculous actions in the world. We tend to ignore those horrible, evil surprises, which for us testify to an absence of God's presence. This absence, too, is a mystery we cannot really understand.

12 There are so many wonders in the world, so many gifts from God to mankind, that our lives are filled with opportunities for learning to love the goodness of God.

13 The mystery of why God created creatures who would use their freedom to turn from God is also beyond our understanding. So is the seemingly divine need for these dramas of repentance in which God's creatures at last understand that they alone cannot rule and direct the universe.

⊠   ⊠   ⊠

30. CREATION AND THE DAY OF REST

1 As creation ordinarily involves effort and struggle, it would seem to by definition be outside the realm of paradise that is the day of rest.

2   As God created the world and then came to rest when
    it was complete, so we in our work stop and rest when
    we finish the products of our creation. Creation is
    understood as the kind of activity that must be
    contemplated in retrospect if it is to be completely
    appreciated. The day of rest is given to us by God so
    that we, too, can appreciate what we have done in the
    six days of the week.

3   Paradise is, according to one interpretation, nothing
    other than the day of rest — the *Shabbat* — the day in
    which we renew our powers so that we will be able to
    create again. But here, too, the analogy between the
    Creator who has power without limitation and the
    creature who creates is a partial and limited one.

4   The day of rest is a reward not only in that we enjoy
    in it the fruits of our labor but also that ideally, we
    contemplate in it the sanctity and beauty of creation
    as a whole.

5   For the religious Jew, the day of rest is also devoted to
    studying the teachings of God. In this activity there is,
    perhaps, a hint of human creation approaching the
    divine in that it paradoxically is most intense on the
    day of rest.

6   On *Shabbat,* the Jew learns to feel that creation is not
    an automatic repetitive act but a free one. The day of
    rest makes the next day of creation one of freedom of
    decision.

7   In the beginning, God could have rested forever and
    not created. That God chose creation and not eternal
    rest is a sign of what He also demands of us.

8   Ideally, each *Shabbat* is the completion of a small
    period of creation and the bridge to a new period of
    creation.

9   Is the ideal end for mankind one long day of rest or one long day of creation? Or, perhaps, is there going to be a time when paradise is nothing other than the creation, which is also rest?

10   *Shabbat* cannot be understood as the cessation of creation but as the moving of creation to a higher level — spiritual creation. The *Shabbat,* then, hints at a messianic time of creation when we will reveal hidden powers in ourselves previously unknown to us.

11   Endless activity would have meant enslaving mankind to its own productivity. The gift of *Shabbat* is the gift of enabling mankind to enjoy the fruit of its labor.

12   The day of rest can be interpreted as the climax of, and most supreme, creation.

13   Six days of the week are intended for work outside the home and in the world. The day of rest is for the home and the family. This day of rest has done more than anything else to sustain the Jewish people in its struggle for survival in the world.

IV

Creation and the Everyday Moral Life

⊠   ⊠   ⊠

31. LIFE AS SACRED TEXT THAT MUST BE READ OVER AND OVER

1 Our lives — our experiences — are God's revelation to us. They are a sacred text that must be read over and over and learned from.

2 Nothing that happens to us is accidental, even the accidental. All has its meaning and should be studied and learned from.

3 The writer, in continually reinterpreting the events of his own life, may come to have a belief that his life is a gift from God, to which he has been chosen to give special and sacred meaning.

4 In rereading one's life — as in rereading a literary text — a page may have one meaning in the beginning and a much different meaning toward the middle or end.

5 There is the revelation given to the entire community through the Torah and the revelation that is the private text of our own lives. These must be read

through each other in order to come to a true understanding of our own reality.

6   In rereading the text of our lives, we often re-create them in order to better understand and solve our present problems.

7   There is a distinction between those who reread their lives to aid them in future action in the world and those who reread them primarily in the hope of re-creating them in literature. For the latter, the true action of their lives is an act of creation that they hope will endure from generation to generation.

8   In rereading one's life, one strives to give it a more lasting significance. Life is not simply that which flows and passes but that which endures by returning. Memory — returning to the past — promises that what has been of great significance once will also be so in the future.

9   By regarding our lives as sacred texts, we live in accordance with the commandment to remember the miracles God has done for us. It is clear that our personal experience contains the experience of the collective as well. Each Jew must, at many times in his life, remember the Exodus from Egypt, from slavery to freedom, the miraculous rescue from the enemy in the crossing of the Red Sea, and the miracle of revelation in receiving the Torah at Sinai.

10 Memory alone is not enough for a certain kind of learning; for higher learning, we need the imagination, which moves us to raise new questions. We need to think about our lives in ways we have not thought of them before. This rereading of our lives may mean

re-creating them in order to better help us realize our purpose in life in serving God.

11 We also makes mistakes, misreadings. Our very act of reinterpretation and re-creation can turn us away from true understanding of the text of our lives. Thus, one important process in the reading is the continual correction made throughout our lives.

12 There are miraculous interventions, signs of God's special care, which help us better understand what direction God wants us to take. God often helps us read the past so as to guide us toward the future.

13 The ideal reading of the text of our lives comes when we sense that what is happening to us is happening just the way we hope it will, just the way God planned it. When it is not happening this way, the great challenge is to remake our lives so that the story is nonetheless one of ideal service of God.

⊠　　⊠　　⊠

32. CREATION AS MAKING ONE'S OWN LIFE IN FREEDOM

1 God commands that we choose good and not evil; God commands that we walk in His ways. God commands that we act in freedom. Thus, the human path in righteousness is creating good for the world through proper use of our freedom.

2   In his daily life decisions, every person has numerous
    opportunities for using his freedom as power of
    creation for good.

3   Our principal use of freedom in our daily lives is in the
    effort to create the good life for ourselves and our
    families.

4   The test of our lives is how we make use of the
    freedom that God gives us, a freedom with which we
    are continually choosing either to walk in God's ways
    or turn from them.

5   One special way we may augment our own freedom is
    through understanding our own limitations and
    striving to overcome them, knowing the weaknesses
    of our own character and resisting them.

6   There are those for whom the creation of experience,
    even the happiest experience, is not true creation.
    There are those who believe they must use their
    freedom to create some kind of work that will con-
    tinue to be meaningful in the generations to come.

7   But we must not forget that the fundamental choice in
    freedom is open to all: whether or not to obey the
    teachings of God. Time and again in Jewish history,
    freedom leads to the wrong choice—sin, disobedi-
    ence, evil, destruction. The golden calf, the wor-
    shiping of idols, occurs again and again in Jewish and
    human history as the direct result of the wrong moral
    choice.

8   Freedom means decision, and decision means risk and
    the possibility of error. This is true even when there is
    good intention and the will to serve God in righteous-
    ness.

9 There are lives events seem to control and people who seem to have no chance. And there are moments in every human life when forces from without are stronger than our own powers of decision and action. These times test our moral character and our faith in God.

10 We often make plans in our lives and act to realize them, only to find that, despite all our efforts, reality has not brought us to where we had hoped. These times when good is not directly rewarded with good are times we are again forced to understand that the way we initially see things may not be the way God sees them in eternity.

11 Only those who have tried to fully make use of their freedom can appreciate how limited that freedom is. Yet it is these people who realize how often action creates new possibilities and that the exercise of freedom creates greater opportunities for freedom.

12 The sin of the modern world is not in making freedom a predominant value but in placing no limit on individual freedom. Such absolutization of the value of freedom has led to the loss of freedom that comes through self-limitation and self-overcoming. It has led to the denial of the distinction between good and evil, a distinction on which all the moral life of mankind is based.

13 The greatest paradox of the moral life is that we are most free when we act in obedience to God, when we do justice, love mercy, and walk humbly with our God.

◻ ◻ ◻

33. TO CREATE OUR OWN DESTINY

1   Creating one's own private life or work according to
    plan is difficult enough. But to create a destiny — that
    is, a life — that will mean something for others' gener-
    ations is so rare as to seem impossible.

2   No one can create his own destiny without the help of
    God. This help often means miraculous intervention
    in the person's life.

3   Creating one's own destiny also means wisely ex-
    ploiting the opportunities that life gives.

4   Creation of a destiny seems to imply long, slow work
    and gradual fulfillment. But what of the poets, war-
    riors, and mathematicians whose destiny is some
    sudden, brief flowering in youth?

5   The kinds of practical maneuvers required to advance
    a career may also be important in creating a destiny.
    Most often the true creator suffers from being so lost
    in his own world of creation that he is inept at
    practical action in the outside world.

6   The life that takes the form of a destiny is the one
    that, in retrospect, looks as if God had planned it
    down to the last detail.

7   There are those who determine to be great before they
    have any idea of what form their greatness will take.
    A vague sense of their own chosenness, specialness,
    haunts them throughout their lives.

8   To make one's own destiny is to make oneself chosen
    by God, to earn God's chosenness through the work
    of our own life.

9   But to make a destiny, it is usually not enough to simply remake a self; it is necessary to create some kind of work that has meaning for others.

10 The great share of mankind is wise enough to not seek for itself a destiny but rather to struggle to make a good life.

11 The ideal life is the one that, when viewed in retrospect, seems as if through it God has added to the justice and mercy in the world.

12 From one perspective, a life of destiny seems inevitable — it is the work and will of God. From another perspective, it seems to be the result of the free action of the person. From the deepest perspective, there is no contradiction between these two.

13 God chooses us in ways we do not know and cannot understand at the time. The suffering, which seems unjust and incomprehensible to us while we live it, often proves to be the force that helped us realize the destiny for which we were chosen.

⊠　　⊠　　⊠

34. CREATION AND EVERYDAY LIFE

1   The moral realm of action in everyday life is the one wherein most people test their own freedom and creative power.

2   In most individuals, there is a desire to be free of freedom and responsibility, to let others take the

burden. This desire wars in us with our desire to be responsible for ourselves.

3   The literary interpretation of a mood or feeling may give it new meaning in the everyday life of the reader. Consider how we may think differently about "indecision and delay" after reading *Hamlet,* or how anxiety takes on a more menacing character when we read the works of Kafka.

4   There is a creative power inherent in every human being. Each human life can be understood as in some sense being a story of what has and has not been created in it.

5   For most people the need for security is stronger than the desire for freedom. Bread and circuses are preferable to painful decision.

6   Most people do not actively choose to do evil, nor, in most cases, do they actively choose to resist it.

7   Danger may increase our inventive power in everyday life.

8   One historical sin of the Jews against God has been our waiting for Him to resist evil for us instead of understanding that the freedom He has given us is His means of helping us in this struggle.

9   The young are, in general, more open than older people to new possibilities. At a certain point in life, people fear going backward far more than they have hope of going forward, and so they do everything possible not to change.

10 The moral test in everyday life is often an internal one. Often our most difficult moral struggles have no

witness but ourselves, and thus provide a special test of our integrity.

11 The kind of creation that is open to most human beings and is also commanded by God is the creation of the generation to come, the making of a family.

12 By our moral action in everyday life, we re-create as well as express our own character. In fact, our whole life story can be understood as an effort at attempted moral perfection of our character.

13 In the Jewish tradition, the central action of goodness in everyday life is in those acts of kindness and mercy called *gemilut hasadem* — visiting the sick, attending the married, supporting the poor, comforting the bereaved: helping others.

▨   ▨   ▨

35. CHOOSING GOOD AND SANCTIFYING EVERYDAY LIFE

1 To choose good, to walk in the way of God, is to create a special blessedness, a sanctity in one's life.

2 There is a pseudoreligion in the modern world built on self-worship and self-indulgence. This permissive giving in to every impulse in the name of false freedom is, in effect, a kind of return to pagan idol worship, whose usual end is the slavery of addiction.

3 The transformation of the evil impulse *(yetzer hara)* into the creative life force is the essence of love. A

Jewish ideal is that in married life love is sanctified and that from this sanctified life comes new life.

4 Lust is transformed into love in the sharing and giving of pleasure in married life.

5 Through marriage, love is made sacred in the service of God.

6 To choose good is to limit one's possibilities in life and in love. Love is sanctified not only by its being with one chosen loved one but also by its being limited in time, and by its having a purpose outside the pleasure of the act itself — the purpose of bringing new life into the world.

7 To choose evil by giving in to one's every impulse is to profane and degrade oneself. But one can also degrade oneself by giving in momentarily to an immediate temptation.

8 To choose good is to consciously strive to serve God in all we do. On one level, it means putting the demand of God before our own pleasure, but on a higher level, it means making the service of God our own supreme pleasure.

9 Creation in imagination can play an important part in preserving and intensifying desire for the person one has chosen to give his lifetime in love.

10 But one must be careful not to worship one's own love lest this, too, become a kind of self-destructive idol.

11 Choosing good is, at one stage, resisting evil and overcoming one's desires. At a higher stage, it is wholeheartedly acting out of the deepest impulse of self — total devotion to good.

12 To love and be loved can be the greatest happiness of life. To give happiness, and from this *know* happiness, can be the sanctification of life in joy.

13 The sanctification of life through service to God is accomplished by being good to and for others. He who does not live for himself alone, but for others and for God, is blessed in righteousness.

▨   ▨   ▨

36. CREATION AND FAMILY LIFE

1 God commands us to create a family, to continue the covenant from generation to generation.

2 Throughout the generations, the central figures of Jewish life have not, as in Christianity, been ascetics but family people. The story of the Jewish people as a whole has been, in a sense, the story of a single family.

3 For the patriarchs and matriarchs of the Jewish people, children came only after a long trial of waiting. They came in such a way as to teach that children are not a product of nature that can be taken for granted but rather a gift of God.

4 Bringing children into the world is only the first step in creating the family. Educating them to walk in God's way is the harder and longer vocation.

5 Human and Jewish history are replete with examples of parents who fail in their children's education. It is remarkable how siblings nurtured by the identical parent example turn out so unlike one another. Cain is not Abel, nor Ishmael Isaac.

6   One crucial test of the success of the Jewish family is whether the grandchildren continue to observe the *mitzvot* so many generations risked their lives to live by.

7   Creative action within the family is that love and mutual help through which the strengthening of one strengthens all. The good and harmonious family is one in which each adult knows how to sacrifice his own selfish interest for the well-being of the family as a whole. This gift often seems lost in the tragic disintegration of many Jewish families in the modern world.

8   The phrase "the child is the center of this life" hints at the family attitude that has provided Jewish children with an especially intense sense of their own value. This has often been translated into the courage to make daring creative efforts in the world.

9   The intergenerational dynamics of Jewish family life has often meant that one generation sacrifices itself to livelihood, business in the world, so that the next generation can devote itself to higher spiritual pursuits.

10 Spiritual creation that is ordinarily thought of in the West as the work of outstanding lonely individuals is often, in Jewish history, the work of whole families. There are Jewish spiritual dynasties of varying kinds. Just a few examples are Rashi and his grandsons, the Baal Shem Tov's family, and the Brisk dynasty of Soloveitchik. These are families that have succeeded

in transmitting the highest level of spiritual creation down through the generations.

11 The connection between the more than ordinary cohesiveness of the Jewish family and the extraordinary creative power of the Jewish people is not incidental. More love within seems to lead to more creation without.

12 In the remarkable battles for survival that the Jewish family has gone through down the generations of exile, the most heroic figure of the family was often the mother. Not only did she raise the children and provide the warmth of the family but she also often provided the means of livelihood so that her husband might devote himself to spiritual pursuits. Her passionate caring is more than anything else responsible for the special blessedness of the traditional Jewish home.

13 The Jewish family, like the Jewish individual, does not have its complete fulfillment in serving itself but must, to truly fulfill itself, serve community and God.

▒   ▒   ▒

37. CREATION AND EVERYDAY WORK LIFE

1 The freer the profession, the greater the creative power required for the work. Doctors and teachers are two kinds of professional workers who must continually exercise their creative powers.

2   The kinds of work that involve the smallest degree of creation — hard physical work and mindless repetitive work — are those mankind holds to be of least value and therefore are rewarded least.

3   The entrepreneur — the individual who acts on his own idea, who risks to build a new enterprise from his own and other people's capital — is for many people the creative figure of the business world. At the same time, there is associated with his activity the sense of ruthless projection of self, which is in contradiction to the Jewish idea of living in service for the community.

4   Literary, academic, even scientific creative activity often involves being enclosed within one's own small world. It is paradoxical, then, that often those who are least worldly change the world most dramatically.

5   The worker who feels his work is contributing to the good of community, who feels his own contribution is understood and appreciated by others, is the one who should, ideally, best serve his society. But often in history the great creative individuals are those who have stood in tension with their community, cultivating ideas that no one is quite ready to understand.

6   The Jews in the diaspora were often deprived of the kind of job security given in regular trades. The Jews were often forced to make some spectacular, extraordinary effort in work that would enable them to make, in a short time, what they could not make in many hours of steady labor.

7   In the modern world, the kind of cultural work that leads to production of a durable product is often held in highest esteem. But when one considers the small number of creative works that truly endure through

the generations one understands how this gift of God can justify the lives of a miniscule minority only.

8   The more creative the work, the greater the risk of failure at it.

9   The kinds of work that involve the highest degree of creative expression are those in which there is the most fierce competition. They are the kinds of work in which repeated rejection is the lot of many.

10   Those who have responsibility over the lives of great numbers of other human beings — the statesmen and the politicians — have greater powers in freedom than most, and also greater burdens in responsibility.

11   There is a strong strain of thought in the Jewish tradition in which it is believed that work is a livelihood only, and the real creative activity is study. There is also the question of whether study alone is enough and whether it compromises its value as service of God through dependency on the work of others.

12   Learning, reading, thinking, studying, and developing oneself are ideals of the creative life. But for many, the real value of such a life can only come in transmitting (often through writing) what one has learned.

13   There is a contradiction between the idea of creation as man's fundamental activity in imitation of God, the Creator, and the idea that work is the punishment for Adam's sin, the burden placed upon mankind in expelling it from paradise. But then mankind can, through making its work a service of God, transform the sinful to the sacred, contribute to the work of correction, *tikkun*, that is the divine redemption of history.

⊠   ⊠   ⊠

38. CREATION GIVES MEANING TO LIFE

1 There are those for whom life without creative work is meaningless.

2 Creation is work, and for a certain kind of person, there is a sense of being truly alive only when working.

3 Rare is the creator whose primary sense of meaning comes from his past achievements, however considerable they may be. Most common is the creator whose sense of meaning is in the work he is doing now or the work he is planning to do next.

4 Is it possible that the true creators have a stronger sense of their own guilt, a greater fear of their own meaninglessness, a more powerful need to justify themselves, than do others?

5 Unending creation without result can bring the creator to despair, for ultimately, the creation, which is for the creator alone, is not *true* creation.

6 Often the meaningfulness of the work for the creator is the sense of having discovered or invented something new, of having brought to the world something that had not existed before.

7 The meaningfulness of the creation is in the interpretations of it, which are made in time. When the creator is no longer present, these interpretations help give meaning to his life.

8   The creation is often conceived by the creator as his means of belonging, his entrance ticket to humanity. How meaningless and empty, then, must he feel when his creation is rejected.

9   Most work in the world is judged meaningful because it earns money. But often the life of the creator takes the form of an investment in himself, which bears no short-term dividends. In the extreme case, this is true even in the creator's lifetime.

10 In his own lifetime, Tolstoy reached both the highest level in literary creation and the highest level of communal recognition; yet, it did not make his life meaningful to him. As opposed to this, it can be suggested that there are many individuals who do work they believe is creative — meaningful to them — but which does not have, and will not have, meaning for mankind.

11 The creator often feels life most meaningful when he is anticipating a great work he dreams to do. And often it is the completion of this work that gives the creator the sense that his life is totally meaningless.

12 No matter how great the recognition in the creator's own lifetime — or even in the generations that come after — there can be no guarantee that the work will truly have ultimate meaning unless God wills it.

13 The creator often creates for the joy of creating, and often because there is nothing else in the world he can do that will give his life meaning or even the hope of meaning.

❖   ❖   ❖

39. THE WORKING OF THE CREATIVE
PROCESS IN EVERYDAY LIFE

1 Often a long process of difficult thinking, a tremendous effort involving tremendous difficulty, is necessary before there comes the sudden flash of intuition
that solves the problem. The suddenness and unex-
pectedness of this intuition give the creator the sense
that the creation is a miracle, a gift that he alone could
not possibly make.

2 Timing is of extreme importance in solving everyday
life problems. "Too soon" can mean creating even
worse problems, and "too late" may mean losing the
chance forever. As Koheleth understood, the wisdom
is in knowing that there is a right and a wrong time for
each and every action we take.

3 Experience often teaches us how to make the right
move, even when we are not consciously directed
toward it. The process of creation, too, involves the
learning of skills and modes of operation that become
part of the repertoire of our very being.

4 Often the only way to see the problem is to listen to
what others think about it. In many good families, the
decision-making process is one of continual consulta-
tion in everyday life.

5 The person often stops just when one small step will
take him out the door to a new world.

6 It is possible to wait—Kafka-like—and make the
smallest problem the source of unending self-torment,
and be unable to do anything about it. Despite all his
effort, the kind of creator each one ultimately is
cannot be determined by himself alone.

7   It is the ability to create new hope, to invent new possibilities when there seem to be none, that is one of the most important skills in maintaining faith in everyday life.

8   Creation in everyday life is often nothing other than choosing and deciding which possibilities to reject.

9   There is a difference between having to make every decision alone and having others to consult with.

10 Life as a whole is a creative process: the decisions we make help create the story line. Those decisions, and the actions we take, most often lead to consequences we have not anticipated, elements of the plot we have no control over. Living means continual rewriting of the story.

11 It is impossible to overestimate the value of good habits and consistent effort in creative work. For even if our work, at times, leads to nothing, our very effort helps move us to the time when new ideas will come.

12 Any answer — even a wrong one — is often better than none at all because it frees the mind, the life, to develop in new directions.

13 The impossible problems we blame God for in the present often prove to be the opportunities and challenges that make our everyday life better in the future. Wisdom, too, can come from persistence in understanding how to wait until God gives us our moment of opportunity.

40. THE INDIVIDUAL'S RE-CREATION OF
HIS OWN MORAL CHARACTER IN
EVERYDAY LIFE

1 One ideal path of moral development begins with the individual thinking only of himself and then moving toward contributing to family, community, and mankind. The path leads from knowing only how to take for oneself to learning how to give to others.

2 Though goodness is primarily the caring and acting for others, this also can be confounded by obsession: there is a kind of being good to others that deprives them of their freedom and power.

3 The best charity is that which helps free the recipient from further need for charity.

4 For many in our world, moral action does not entail great risk; rather it entails overcoming the reluctance to take some minor discomfort upon oneself.

5 What is easy at first often provides the greatest difficulties later; what requires painstaking effort in the beginning often turns to smooth sailing later. The moral character is strengthened by taking on the harder things and overcoming them.

6 It is moral to demand first of oneself, and then set the example that may hopefully lead others to follow.

7 There is a goodness that naturally flows from the very being of the person, and there is a goodness in which the individual must continually strive to overcome his own evil impulses.

8 There are those who understand that the more they help others, the more they help themselves. But this is not true when their only real intention is helping themselves.

9   Job does everything right, is grateful for the blessing he is given, and is perfectly moral and upright. Suddenly, righteousness is not rewarded and evil tests him. He maintains a higher morality and integrity before God, while at the same time protesting in silence. But then he hears the voice in the whirlwind and understands that there is a reality beyond even his own greatest pain or blessing.

10   The fear of punishment is with many of us from childhood. Even in our adult life, we often do good because we know that doing evil will bring evil to us.

11   It is possible to think of a creator driven by two contradictory goals. On the one hand, he wants to re-create his life as one of moral righteousness in service to God. On the other hand, he wants to exalt his own name in greatness through his own creation. Only a long life of struggle, failure, and humiliation can bring him to the understanding that only if he achieves the moral perfection of serving God first will his own name be exalted.

12   One great fear of those who must re-create their characters in righteousness is the understanding that to do this, they must learn not only to contradict themselves but also to fight against others in the world.

13   In youth we try to and fail to conquer life through serving only ourselves. In later years we come to the wisdom that only through giving to others will our own lives be blessed.

V

Creation and the Life of the Mind

❈   ❈   ❈

41. INTERPRETING, UNDERSTANDING, AND RE-CREATING REALITY

1 In order to know and understand ourselves, we must know and understand the world.

2 In understanding human life, the truth is often an interpretation we choose to make. Truth, in this sense, is not a matter of contemplation or discovery but a matter of judgment and decision.

3 Humanistic interpretation is possibly open-ended and unending. Therefore, it is rare that the truth in humanistic studies is a single interpretation that is proved absolutely right.

4 Interpretation is re-creation; therefore, knowing the truth is often dependent on acts of the imagination. Knowing the truth is also, in this sense, an aesthetic activity.

5 Contradictory truths in humanistic discourse often complement one another to make a more complex, confusing, yet truer picture of reality. Not either/or but both/and is very often the truth.

6 Our lives can be reread endlessly so as to make them seem an infinite chaos of meaning. Therefore, wisdom is in knowing how to choose the meaning we need to live the good life and then strengthening this with additional example and interpretation.

7 Interpreting the truth is an act of human decision and freedom, another means of creation by which we can do the work of God in the world.

8 We often encounter a truth in the external world just as we are creating such a truth inwardly.

9 Attaining a true understanding of reality is a long process of learning that involves the making of many decisions. In other words, the whole process of knowing the truth is also part of our struggle in freedom to make our own lives. Knowing the truth is, then, part of our own personal story of creation.

10 Different levels of reality coexist and interact in such a way that the true picture of the world must include worlds within worlds and worlds beyond our understanding. In all our acts of intellectual discovery there should be a place for humility, for understanding how small a part of all of God's creation we can know. The intellectual process of knowing the truth in the world thus ideally leads us in humility to a religious understanding of humanity's relation to God.

11 There is a kind of creator who lives to know the truth and who suffers in knowing that this truth will not be some single, definite answer but an unending reinterpretation, much of which will come into being only

when he has left the world. But the insult of igno-rance, which such a creator suffers in youthful arro-gance for conquest, can with age become a more resigned understanding of how humanity must ulti-mately rely on God as the One who finally under-stands everything.

12 Human life is often a battleground of conflicting interpretations of reality, of differing versions of the same event. Thus, knowing the truth often takes the form of creating an argument to support one's own position.

13 The truth is not simply a memory—it is a map, and we are constantly re-creating new guidelines by which we can practically make our way in the world. This occurs even when we have one basic map, the Torah, that guides us in everything.

⊠   ⊠   ⊠

42. HISTORY AS A STRUGGLE FOR CONTROL OF THE CONSCIOUSNESS OF MANKIND

1 Faith communities and cultural communities struggle to make their respective visions of the world the central and predominant belief system of mankind.

2 Jews, Christians, and Muslims struggle against one another to prove that the One Creator is on their side, though each believes that in the end mankind will be united in the worship of One God. The Jews, how-

ever, do not believe the whole world will have to
become Jewish for this to happen.

3 All these struggles for predominance in belief can be
seen as part of God's plan for the world, great parts of
which are necessarily hidden from us. Many of us
have more difficulty making logical and moral sense
of what we know of the world than of what we do not
know.

4 The struggle for human consciousness is the struggle
to understand what will be preserved and remembered
from generation to generation. The cruelty of life is,
in one sense, that every present victory is only tem-
porary and the real test will take place in future
generations when we are not here to witness it.

5 Contradiction, debate, capacity for arguing in favor
of one's own view, chaos of visions, no single unified
system of belief—some believe this to be the ideal
situation for mankind. There would be no triumph of
a single vision but the ongoing contest for truth. This
pluralistic vision of the world places a supreme value
on human freedom of inquiry. It is precisely in this
kind of world that the Jewish vision must today make
its argument and struggle and so speak to the power
of freedom, thought, and creation in the mind of the
individual Jew.

6 Deep within the Jewish tradition—in fact, a constitu-
tive element of that tradition—is a process of endless
inquiry and questioning, endless debate for clarifica-
tion and extension of meaning. The capacity for
accommodating a variety of interpretations around a
basic system of truth is essential to the Jewish tradition in thought.

7   There are realms of inquiry in which the struggle for truth is open only to the small number of experts qualified to understand the subject. Yet these realms of truth are often universal and often have the greatest influence on the scientific and technical development of mankind.

8   It is not only that the truth (or the best approximation to it) is power. It is that power makes the truth. The conquering community imposes its vision of the world on others. History is full of examples of backward peoples who conquer an advanced civilization and succumb to its way of understanding the world.

9   The Christians and Muslims have convinced a good share of the world of the necessity of worshiping one and only one God. But historically, they have by and large refused to think of their vision of God as complementing that first revealed to Israel. Rather, they have tried to spiritually conquer Israel by arguing that their vision has replaced ours.

10   The very same events are reinterpreted by successive generations of scholars in various ways. The most definitive interpretation of a subject today is likely to be replaced by a more definitive version later.

11   The struggle for the consciousness of mankind is also a struggle between different activities and areas of thought. Thus, civilization was once at a stage where the religious vision determined everything, including the scientific and the technical. Now, religion often seems to be just one more specialized area of intellectual and academic inquiry.

12   Understanding complicated scientific and intellectual visions of the world as part of the creation of God is

a way of augmenting the Jewish religious vision of the world.

13 Is mankind moving toward a vision of democratic freedom, and justice under God, a synthesis of the best Western secular and Jewish religious ideals?

⊠   ⊠   ⊠

43. KNOWING EVERYTHING AND CREATING A TRUE PICTURE OF THE WORLD

1 It is possible to spend a lifetime trying to know everything. But in one day in the life of mankind more information is gathered and lost than any individual can hope to collect in his lifetime.

2 Once we understand that we cannot know everything, we strive to know what is most essential, what is most true, most good, most beautiful. We make a decision—consciously or not—to select and choose, and in this way we begin to re-create reality.

3 The act of knowing—as are the acts of selecting, learning, making hypotheses, testing and weighing evidence, choosing between alternative explanations, inventing new possibilities to explain former realities—is an act of creation. We grow not simply by re-creating ourselves but also by continually re-creating, learning, and knowing the world.

4 At a certain age, we become wise enough to understand not only that we will not know everything but also that it may not be so important that we do not.

For those who have loved truth from childhood, such a revelation can be as disappointing as it is surprising.

5   A great artist makes a picture of the world and so creates a world of his own. In some way this world is more *and* less real than the real world. Yet, if the artist is great, the picture, too, becomes part of reality, transforming and enriching it, making it even more complicated and unknowable.

6   When we understand that we cannot make a true picture of reality in all its detail, we search for a way of comprehending it in general terms, through a broad outline. We make systems of abstractions through which we summarize reality. But this does not give us everything, for we cannot subsume one realm or language of discourse with another. The outline of philosophy is not the song of poetry, and the vision of astronomy is not the perception by our eyes — much less our hearts — of the stars.

7   The making of many models or pictures of reality at different times of one's life — even from the perspective of others — helps us realize that completeness of understanding is not a goal to ever be finally realized but one to be approached again and again as closely as possible.

8   Aesthetically, a factually accurate picture of the world is not, in itself, true enough. The artist's picture of the world must move us to assent to it as a kind of revelation; otherwise, it is meaningless. In this sense, for the artist, the true picture of the world is the one he creates, which others come to believe in.

9   Re-creation is never imitation or representation in and by itself. But without some kind of representation, most re-creation loses its human appeal.

10 There are those who, understanding that they cannot understand everything, believe their intellectual integrity is in admitting they understand nothing. For them, to not know everything is to not know anything at all. But this kind of integrity is, while acceptable on a theoretical level, unrealistic and self-defeating on the level of everyday practicality.

11 Very often we feel we understand reality when we make a picture in our minds. Thus, the Jewish understanding of God as One who cannot be reduced to an image is one that means the basic vision of the world is informed by—even dominated by—mystery.

12 Better to make one small creation, which will be part of the world of others, than to live alone with the vast understanding of what others will never know.

13 The creator moves from the hope of understanding all, which is, in effect, the hope of seeing the world the way God sees it, to the hope of contributing to others' vision of the world, which is, in effect, the serving of God in his own small way.

⊠   ⊠   ⊠

44. THE PLACE OF CONTRADICTION IN ANY UNDERSTANDING WE HAVE OF ULTIMATE REALITY

1 Life and reality are such that we inevitably find ourselves believing in contradictory truths.

2   One contradiction most Jews implicitly believe is that God has commanded us to be free and that we must be free if we are to realize God's plan for us.

3   When our understanding of some fundamental question concerning our relation to God leads us to impossible contradictions, we begin to understand the limits of our own understanding and reason.

4   We often have a sense that in readily believing contradictory truths, we are compromising our intellectual integrity, and that in deferring intellectually to the Transcendent Mystery, we are accepting too readily the contradiction between the creature created in God's image, unable to know that image, and the Creator who knows all.

5   We cannot reconcile the belief in God's absolute goodness and power with our personal knowledge of evil in the world. We resolve this contradiction by turning to a higher world, by relying on God's incomprehensibility, or in some cases, by understanding that the knowledge we have at one stage of life is not necessarily that which we will have at another.

6   Even philosophers do not die of contradictions: the perfectly rational is not all of life and for most, not even the major part of it.

7   If we love the truth, the inescapability of ultimate contradiction disturbs us and this leads, in turn, to another contradiction—that we must trust God and strive for peace of mind when we have reason for not believing in the rightfulness of such peace.

8   Fundamental religious contradictions result from our need to believe that God cares for us. For there is

evidence in the world that suggests that we are of no ultimate significance, that chaos rules the world, that chance and accident make our destiny.

9   God did not construct the world in such a way as to make reason the supreme arbiter in all searches for truth. God did not create for each and every question a clear, rational answer.

10   There are times when experience presents such strong contradiction to our faith in the goodness of God and His love of mankind that we can bring ourselves to no other reaction than silence. For even the thought, "Also this is for good," is at these times not able to console us.

11   There is the intellectual temptation to explain away all contradiction and make of reality a single, consistent, and coherent system. But real intellectual courage may well be in resisting such simplistic systems and living with the inconsistencies, no matter how difficult this is.

12   There live within us contradictory views of reality formed at different stages of our lives by different kinds of thoughts. We bear these contradictions as our truth and trust that if we cannot resolve them by ourselves, one day God will help us resolve them.

13   All the contradictions we come to in striving to understand the ultimate nature of God do not change the truth that God is the One on whom we are dependent for the salvation of all we love.

45. MAKING A TRUE PICTURE OF THE WORLD THROUGH RE-CREATION OF VARIOUS "TIMES"

1   Each person is limited in knowledge by the limited interval of time in which he lives. The greatest part of the past and the future is beyond his direct experiencing.

2   Each generation creates its own picture of the world, including its picture of how other generations see it and how it sees other generations. Each and every one of these pictures is incomplete and fragmentary in relation to the whole truth.

3   The more time we give to re-creating a phase or time of our own life, the more that time becomes central to our picture of the world. But this choice of a time is one that neglects and ignores most other times and so helps deepen the incompleteness and subjectivity of our necessarily incomplete and subjective picture of the world.

4   Even if one creates a more vast panorama of a generation than anyone has ever done before (e.g., Balzac), it is still incomplete and small before the hidden reality of that time, much of which is destined for oblivion.

5   Every re-creation of a past time is the saving of a small remnant of it.

6   The desire to know all past times, to understand all experience, is another of the human efforts to understand God the Creator from both inside and outside at once. It is another of the human efforts, always

bound to fail, to see the whole through the eyes of God.

7   It is possible to reimagine the inner life and time of another person, as one does with a literary character. But most often the characters who live in literature are composite creations based in some way on a number of real people and transformed uniquely by the author. That such characters live in the reader's memory for generations when the vast majority of mankind does not is another of God's interesting surprises for us in history.

8   More times live in us, more past worlds of our own private experience, than we can possibly be conscious of at any one time. And even those who make a deliberate effort at re-creating such time know that only a small part of what they have experienced will be re-created in their work. Thus, we are all — even the greatest human creators — always small fragments of our own lives, experiences, memories, and selves.

9   The memory of a past time of our life, and the re-creation of it as literature, can give us the sense of restoring a lost world. This may be one of the most significant of all human experiences, however fictional and incomplete it may be.

10 To go back and recall a past time is often to feel oneself alive at more than one time at once. It is to feel the multiplicity of one's own self. While disturbing and disconcerting in one sense, this can provide greater depth and wonder to one's experience of oneself.

11 The creator who re-creates different times is extending his own life and mind, re-creating himself and his

world. He does this not only out of a disinterested desire for knowledge but also out of a sinful desire to possess all worlds of experience as only God may possess them.

12   To know reality from outside dryly and objectively provides one kind of understanding. But to know reality from inside, through reimagining the life and experience of others, provides a deeper knowledge of the human world. This kind of living from inside is what gives great literary creators their power to move and inspire us.

13   To experience from inside the life of every human being who has ever lived — to know each and every life and time from the point of view of every other one — is yet another kind of divine omnipotence the human mind cannot truly conceive of. Only the mind of God can make a picture of the world that includes all lives and all times.

⌗   ⌗   ⌗

46. RE-CREATING THE LIVES OF OTHERS

1   We strive to re-create the lives of others so that we can, in some sense, become them and in this way expand our own being. In this, too, we strive unsuccessfully to imitate God.

2   To try and experience the lives of others from inside is to try and help complete our own necessarily imperfect picture of the world. It is to try and gain more

evidence so as to help us solve the mysteries of our lives and characters.

3   The attempt to understand the world of others from inside is the attempt to possess those lives and selves as our own. And this when ultimately we do not even possess ourselves but belong only to God.

4   If experiencing is taken to be the highest human good, then knowing the world of others from inside is a way of increasing the goodness of our own lives. But in the Jewish tradition, not all experience is to be sought after; in fact, much of it is to be avoided, even if this means struggling against our own desires.

5   The impulse to know the inner world of another can be an impulse in evil or an impulse in good. Most often we want to know other people's thoughts and feelings in order to properly care for them. And if they are people we love, knowing them most closely can be a way of helping them in their own lives and decisions.

6   We may think we know another from inside, but just as we often surprise ourselves with new thoughts, so the minds of others are usually working to create new realities. Freedom means that even those we love most and think we know best can surprise us in ways we are not necessarily happy with.

7   It is possible to imagine the making of a record of every type of human character. This record would be part of humanity's effort to know and understand itself. But this record, too, must be incomplete so long as human beings are free and capable of creating new lives and selves (even new characters) for themselves in the future.

8   Every re-creation of the inner world of others is a kind
    of fiction based on conjecture. For there is only one
    self each one of us knows intimately, one self we live
    with, moment to moment, in our own individual
    minds.

9   The question of how God can know each human
    being from inside without also knowing his evil
    impulses and actions is, in essence, no different from
    the question of how God can be the Creator of good
    and evil while at the same time being purely and
    absolutely good.

10 What if knowing others from inside does not bring us
    the greater closeness and understanding we originally
    hope for but instead reveals to us a world of hidden
    evil intentions. What if there is great wisdom in God's
    having constructed us in such a way that we can only
    intimately know the evil impulses of one person—
    ourselves?

11 One form of creation is to know others in our
    imagination and to re-create their lives there. But
    when this leads to our interfering in their lives in the
    real world, the creator may sin in using his freedom to
    deprive others of theirs.

12 The kind of systematic effort made in creating a
    character in literature often leads to a more complete
    knowledge of others than is usually gained in our
    more fragmentary apprehensions in everyday life.

13 It is one thing to wish to know the character of
    another in order to help him, and another to wish to
    know simply for our own curiosity. Part of caring for
    others is knowing when not to try to know them too
    much. We must remember that our goal in learning

about another should be the service of God and of His
creations.

⊠   ⊠   ⊠

47. TO KNOW ONESELF

1   In both the flow of our consciousness and in action,
we are continually re-creating ourselves.

2   We know ourselves from inside as no one else can.
This special relationship is with us all the time, though
we become conscious of it only at special moments of
reflection.

3   When we experience our own creative power in
speech, or in reaction to others in the world, we know
there is a dimension of ourselves that is forever
unknown and unpredictable, even to us. We cannot
know ourselves completely, and this ignorance too is
an element of our freedom.

4   At times we seek to remember what we were, but we
feel so far from our past selves that it seems as if we
were then a completely different person.

5   We can create ourselves in a lifetime of effort and
then suddenly lose ourselves to an illness or through
the loss of a loved one. In other words, some aspect of
our self requires constant reaffirmation if it is to
continue to exist.

6   An earlier time, which may have been the best time of
our lives, may be mourned by us. And in this mourning, it is as if we grieve for our own lost self.

7   Whatever we know of ourselves is never an adequate substitute for real love by some member of our family.

8   At a certain point we are aware of so many aspects of our own character that we are able to choose the self we presently wish to be. At the same time, we retain the real and undivided self, which contrasts with the possible selves with which we play the game of life with others. This raises the question not only of which self God judges but also which self God will ultimately choose to make real in the other world.

9   To know oneself for all one's potential selves is also to know the evil in oneself. Ideally, this should lead us to penitence in quest of the purer self we might become.

10 Knowing oneself for the human being is not simply a matter of understanding one's own past; it is a question of creating one's own future. It is important for us to have an ideal of the righteous self — the good person we wish to be — that we can strive for. In the Jewish tradition that person does justice, loves mercy, and walks humbly with his God.

11 The great cultural creator often has an idea in his mind of how future generations will regard him. He has a sense of an ideal self who will endure beyond his own lifetime. He knows himself as a dream of what he will be in the minds and hearts of others when he is no longer present to experience it.

12 No matter how we may disappoint ourselves in life, we should always understand ourselves as loved by God. And this knowledge should be our faith and strength in hope of better times to come.

13   We know ourselves so well, and yet we continually
surprise ourselves. In other words, the miracle of the
freedom God has given us is ever present in our daily
lives and minds, if only we can appreciate it.

⊠   ⊠   ⊠

48. THE CREATION OF AN IDEAL SELF

1   There is a kind of creator who invents various styles
or characters as a way of multiplying and extending
the self as many, when underneath it all there is
ordinarily one voice and signature only. Here, too,
the human creator strives to imitate the Creator and,
in understanding his own limitations, comes to a
deeper appreciation of the One True Creator.

2   To create one's ideal self, one must be prepared not
only to know disappointments but also to recover
from these disappointments, even make opportunities
of them. The ideal self is understood not as a stagnant
or fixed entity but as a story in creation.

3   The creation of an ideal self is often achieved through
participation in a common myth. One such myth is
that of the long-suffering, much-rejected creator who
is recognized only after he has left this world. Another
such myth is that of the heroic creator who, Jacob-
like, struggles with the angel of God and wins his
people's true name.

4   The ideal self is most often created not when the self
is taken as object but when the ideal is some goal in
the world. The creator re-creates himself through his

work. So, too, each person re-creates himself through the deeds of his life and their effect on others.

5   Unexpected consequences, errors in decision, terrible surprises from without all interfere with the enterprise of living one's life in accordance with one's plan, being true to the ideal self one has chosen for oneself. Persistence and faith must be central elements in the character of one who walks in God's ways. The ability to find answers for oneself, which no one else can provide, is also an important element.

6   The ideal creator is totally devoted to making a work that serves God and the people of Israel and at the same time is devoted to achieving the most supreme aesthetic level in creation. The ideal creator's demands upon himself are maximum, while at the same time he has the deepest possible awareness of the limitations of any human creation.

7   It is possible to imagine a person who is so busy doing good in the world that he has no time to wonder about creating his own ideal self. His ideal self is the real life he lives in service of others.

8   There are many varieties of the ideal self given in the Jewish tradition—from patriarch to prophet, from talmid chacham to hasid. There are many past examples, which can serve as models in the present life, for creating the ideal self. And yet, as no life can be the exact duplicate of another, each one must go through his own struggles and temptations, his own overcoming of self, to create the ideal self.

9   There is always the danger that in living to create one's own ideal self, one will worship himself rather than

God. And this when our task is to make our love of
ourselves a basis for our much more profound love of
God.

10   Imagine a creator whose own sense of self diminishes
as his creation grows greater and greater. Imagine a
creator in humility whose knowledge and wisdom
grow in direct proportion to his sense of how there
can be only One Creator who can truly order the
world.

11   The ideal self is almost always one part of a more
complex and compromised self.

12   The modern romantic concept of the ideal self as one
who experiences everything often leads the person to
self-degradation and destruction.

13   To create one's own ideal self is to test oneself in
freedom. This is a task that continues throughout the
person's life, even through old age.

⊠   ⊠   ⊠

49. A KIND OF IDEAL CREATOR: THE IN-BETWEEN MAN

1   The ideal creator does not fit easily into any category.
His connection with each and every tradition of
creation is incomplete. The kind of in-between creator, who is not easily classifiable, has no certain
place but the new and unique place he makes for
himself.

2   When one belongs nowhere, one is forced to make a category of one's own name; one is forced to have the world build a discipline and tradition around one's own individual creation.

3   The in-betweenness of the creator's position also reflects his whole sense of the way the world is constructed. For him, knowing the world can never be an exercise in simply grasping the whole truth. The truth is also a complicated composition of partial truths, a conglomeration of diverse and mixed categories changing in time.

4   The in-betweenness also means the creator lacks the kind of totalitarian mind that knows the whole of reality and predicts it perfectly to others.

5   The in-betweenness is also between the need to be true to the Jewish religious tradition and the demand for secular learning. This means there is a dividedness in time with in-between man, who is never wholly able to give his time to one and only one way of knowing. He is called—tempted—in both directions, with his only consolation being the idea that all real learning is the service of God.

6   The in-between man dreams that by creating the tradition of his own name, his work will later be embraced by traditions that have previously rejected it and that they will then see his work as an extension of their own tradition. But he is also aware of the possibility that his work may never fit in traditions he dreams it will be a part of.

7   The in-between creator has his mind and eye on the specific situation, the actual experience, but he is also looking for a way of ordering reality through abstract

classification. His being between the ever-changing, specific situations of life and the fixed categories of abstract thought also marks his in-between incompleteness.

8   In-between man writes history — which is really more philosophy than history — and literature — which is more religion than art. There is always a mixture of categories in whatever he does.

9   In-betweenness reflects the pull of different worlds and identities. The Jew in America may be more a Jew or more an American, but he is shaped by both identities. The Jew in Israel may feel his identity formed by the various diasporas his ancestors wandered through. For the in-between man, "identity" is a mosaic of components, and he himself decides which are to be made prominent, focused on, and developed.

10 In its negative sense, in-betweenness is an inability to be wholly committed to one tradition; it means a state of perpetual indecision. Or, in a positive sense, it is a perpetual need to make a decision.

11 The Jews have most often in their history been in more than one place when in only one place. All the years of exile, their hearts and aspirations were in Israel. Yet even when in Israel, in Jerusalem there are two worlds, two places — the lower Jerusalem of ordinary life and the higher Jerusalem of spiritual aspiration.

12 In-between man searches to integrate worlds — secular and religious, Hellenic and Hebraic — but the integration is usually a mixture of contradictory and opposing realities. Truth is a tension that cannot be resolved, a set of incompletenesses moving to a higher stage of completeness.

13   Because of his awareness of the partial and limited
     character of all he sees and does, in-between man
     (ideally) walks with humility through the world.

⧅   ⧅   ⧅

50. CREATION AND THE HIDDEN POWERS
OF THE SELF

1   At the heart of freedom of action, there is always a
    need for some larger help from within and without.
    No free human action is possible without the comple-
    mentary help of God.

2   The creation of a work of art is like our free action in
    life and history in that it often takes a shape and
    consequence beyond our initial conception of it.

3   Often the creator's feeling is, "I am not creating; God
    is creating within me."

4   At the height of creation, the creator feels that all his
    inner powers are being employed, that the whole of
    his being is making the creation, that at last he is
    doing what God put him on this earth to do.

5   At the time of true creation, the creator feels most
    alive. As in love, so in creation—when all is right,
    there is nothing more that one could ask of life.

6   The understanding that in creating, one is relying on
    powers that are somehow not really his own, creates a
    humility in the creator. He knows his work is a gift of
    God, a blessing for which he must be grateful.

7 It takes years of preparation and hard work to bring forth the most powerful kinds of action in creation.

8 In creation there is a process of deciding for oneself that is not based on calculation or rationality. It comes out of an inner feeling, an intuition, a trusting in deep faith of one's own inner self, as if God is there when the creator needs Him. In this way, creation can be for the individual both an expression of and proof of religious faith.

9 The creator must make repeated efforts and fail repeatedly until the point comes when suddenly the dream of creation is realized effortlessly.

10 We learn by imitating the work of other creators, but God has created each of us in such a way that we cannot be anyone but ourselves. This means that our failures, too, must bear our own unique signature.

11 The process of making an effort, failing, making another effort, then suddenly realizing not this present dream of creation but one from long ago is another gift of surprise in creation. Sometimes God rewards us unexpectedly in ways that show us how right we were in our persistence.

12 All the will in the world will not bring forth true creation unless God grants us the inner power.

13 In time, the master creator develops a repertoire of skills and styles that he can put to use when the occasion demands. And yet, the spark of the highest creation can never be part of that repertoire. Deeper than the deepest self is the inspiration that transforms the ordinary work into one of greatness. This is a process of chosenness that no creator can master, and it depends on God and God alone.

VI

Literary Creation

❇   ❇   ❇

51. CREATION IN LIFE AND/OR LITERATURE

1 The life of the creator will not endure. The creation of the literature, when it centers on the life, dreams to make the life endure in the imagination and memory of future generations. Thus, there are creators who care less for what they experience in life than for what they create in art. This, too, may mean that the creator cares more for his creation in art than for his happiness in life.

2 It may be moral to sacrifice one's own life for literary creation. But can it be moral to sacrifice the lives of one's loved ones for such creation?

3 There is no case of a great creator who made perfection of both life and work. But then, as the lives of our greatest prophets and teachers show, there is no perfect life in and of itself either.

4 The great creator may appear for a certain time of his life so completely dedicated to his creation as to be a

slave of it. But the great creators in medieval Jewish
religious thought (Rambam, Ramban, Saadia Gaon,
Rashi) always had public and communal duties, business that required their moving from one activity to
another and prevented them from ever being lost in a
single narrow routine.

5 Jewish creators through the generations have managed
to balance family life with spiritual creation. This is
because their family life and the education of their
children was an essential part of their spiritual work.

6 This is another meaning of *Shabbat:* the rest from
work means preventing oneself from becoming en-
slaved by it.

7 The spiritual creation of generations of Jews had its
principal expression not in what was written down for
them to learn in reading but in what was taught orally.
Lives were given to works that had little literal remembrance. Yet great teachers are kept alive in the tradition
through the continuing study of their students.

8 The idea of the creator somehow existing indepen-
dently of any public framework, of somehow working
on his own in total dedication to his own imagined
idea of a vast reading public, is a phenomenon of the
modern world that has led many individuals to disaster. For the Jewish creator, such a situation expresses
loss of connection and integration with traditional
Jewish meaning and interpretation.

9 There is a kind of creator who so strongly senses his
work is a gift of God that he cannot stop himself from
creating new work, even if he has had small success in
the past and little prospect of great worldly success in
the future.

10 In the modern world, where such a vast majority of the Jewish public has a secular rather than a Jewish religious education, one ideal creator would work to return his people to their tradition. One way this might be done is by setting an example in life and creation that can be an inspiration to those who would develop their interest in the sources of the tradition.

11 It is possible to imagine a kind of creator who has lived and worked for himself and his own name alone and who fails and fails until he is slowly brought to understand that only through service of God, only through work done for the name of God, will his own life know its justification.

12 It is at the time of most intense creation, when the creator is doing the work he has struggled all his life to do — lived all his life to arrive at — that the creator is most alive.

13 The process of creation can be, for the creator, the single central means of making meaning in life. It can be the renewal of hope in life; it can be the time of being closest to God and sanctifying life by living it in accordance with God's purpose for it.

⊠   ⊠   ⊠

52. THE WRITER'S IMMORTALIZATION OF THOSE HE LOVES THROUGH LITERATURE

1 For one kind of writer, the central task of his work is to immortalize those he loves in literature. It is to ensure that their departure from this world will not be final and that they will live forever in the hearts and minds of generations to come. This raises the question as to what this expresses about the writer's trust that God will save all in the world-to-come.

2   As the great mass of mankind dies into oblivion, the writer tries to immortalize those he loves for future generations, tries to choose them for a kind of world-to-come. It is as if he does not have trust in God's world-to-come.

3   There is something suspect about the love that is given in immortalizing the real-life person in literature. For what kind of gift can this be when the one who is to receive it does not know of it and cannot appreciate and enjoy it?

4   The loss of a loved one may move the writer to attempt to immortalize him or her in literature because he believes this is his only means of helping. This effort at immortalization comes out of a desperate desire to keep alive what is already gone.

5   Most writers of great distinction have succeeded less in immortalizing loved ones than they have in immortalizing themselves and their fictional characters.

6   There are characters we have known in real life who seem so great as to make even the most devoted literary effort at their immortalization appear small and inadequate.

7   The writer who wishes to immortalize a loved one may, like a painter, make repeated efforts at the same subject, at different stages of life. It is as if the artist's

remembrance is also a sequence of stages, a history of all the ways his subject can be known.

8   The great sages are remembered generation to generation. There are thousands of individuals who have made some distinct and unique contribution to Jewish history for which they are remembered. But the great majority of Jews have lived in memory for only one or two generations after their passing, even though their loved ones had faith that the souls of the righteous ascend and that all Israel has a place in the world-to-come.

9   It is as if in seeking to supplement the life in the divine world-to-come with the creation of his own world-to-come, the writer expresses his own doubt and insecurity about the reality of immortality. This doubt and insecurity might come from a close reading of a certain part of the Jewish tradition and an understanding that what matters for the biblical characters is what they are in this world alone.

10 In establishing a name that will live for centuries, the great literary creator often casts a shadow on his own family. Instead of making them great in the minds of others, he makes them — with or without intention — bit players who serve him, the protagonist of the drama.

11 One method for building an immortal picture of a real-life character is through re-creating him in reference to a whole combination, a vast array of previous literary characters, each of whom is some small part of him.

12 Another method for immortalizing a real-life character might be by using him as basis for a fictional

character of great power. But this kind of remembrance is small and ultimately unable to do justice to
some real person who has been loved in the world.

13 The great figures of biblical literature live not only
through their descendants, not only through their
lives in some higher other world, but also in human
memory generation to generation. They are a chosen
few out of the vast number of human beings who have
lived on this earth only to be completely forgotten a
generation or two after their deaths.

❈   ❈   ❈

53. CREATION AND THE STRIVING OF THE CREATOR FOR HIS OWN IMMORTALIZATION

1 For the prophets, the direct revelation of the teachings
of God meant confronting mankind. They did not
speak for themselves but for God. The prophets, who
are immortal in the Jewish tradition, did not strive to
immortalize themselves but rather to serve God.

2 Often, the creator aims to be worshiped from generation to generation, as if the work were done only for
the exaltation of his own name. This exclusive worship of the self is sin.

3 Only God can be conceived as going beyond all time
to preserve what has been in time. Thus, even for
the most individualistic and self-centered of thinkers,
the only real hope for ultimate immortalization is the
service of God.

4 How does the individual creator know he is not using his service of God as means for first serving himself? How can he know that his love for the name of God is truly greater than his love for his own individual name? Perhaps he can know by understanding what is included in the name of God (including those he loves), which cannot be included in his name alone.

5 Is there any guarantee that the great cultural creators of mankind are loved by God as they are by the generations of humanity? Isn't it just as likely that God cares for those countless individuals who have lived lives of goodness, who have been kind and caring for others although no one noticed or made great mention of this in their lifetimes or afterward?

6 Among the immortals of mankind there are many who are monstrously evil, especially in the military and political realms. These great creators of human history are remembered by mankind now, which seems a terrible injustice when their victims are, by and large, nameless to posterity. Here again, we must rely on the world-to-come if we are to hope for justice.

7 One reason cultural creators have striven with such determination for the recognition of mankind is that they have ceased to believe in a God who cares for them. Immortality, which comes of being remembered by human posterity, may be a poor substitute, but for many it is the only possible substitute for the eternal love of God.

8 Does the righteous and just man have to strive for immortality through cultural creation? Isn't it clear

that, in biblical terms, his being good, just, and
merciful is what he will be rewarded for?

9 The creator may seem to strive for immortalization in
another world when his real torment is over justification in this one.

10 The striving for immortalization may be but one of
the creator's goals: he may also strive to immortalize
those he loves to advance his own practical goals in
making an everyday life of happiness. He may also
strive to love and serve God. And it may be that his
inner struggle is to turn what appears to be a sin of
Faustian self-worship into a small part of his overall
complex inner yearning to do good and serve God.

11 The same creator who at one point believes his only
goal is the struggle for immortality can, at another
time, sense his real aim is to belong to a certain world
of creation or community of meaning. His aim is to
escape the terrible isolation of his own life.

12 The more the individual creator returns to trust in
God and the Jewish tradition, the deeper the sense
that his own life and work are not in vain but are part
of God's plan for him.

13 The creator who creates with joy both in the work and
in the intention of serving God may find in the work
itself the only immortality he needs. He may in his
consciousness of serving God wholeheartedly be free
of the fear that his life and work might not be
remembered.

⊠   ⊠   ⊠

54. LOVE AND CREATION

1   The great creator is often a child striving for the love of a parent who never completely approves.

2   In demanding recognition, praise, and love for his name, the creator walks in the way of God. But when that name becomes more important than the name of God, there is sin in his creation.

3   At the moment of intense joy in creation, when the true work is being done, there is a real sense of discovery and revelation and with it, often an over-powering gratitude to God.

4   The ideal creator would have the service, the love, and the fear of God continually before him and would always be striving to serve the name of God.

5   In love, as in creation, there is a point where compulsive giving—giving without demanding anything in return—leads to humiliation and self-defeat.

6   God's fundamentally positive attitude toward creation, God's love of His children, should be the example that guides the creator in all his work.

7   There is a kind of higher creation in secular literature (Tolstoy's *War and Peace* is perhaps the best example) that inspires love of life and wonder at the miracle of human existence. It inspires the desire to live and be part of the world.

8   One path of ideal development for the true creator is to move from living a life dominated by fear and self-torment to living one in which the fear of God is no greater than the love of God. This kind of path might be taken by the creator who has learned to

accept life's responsibilities, know suffering, struggle to overcome that suffering, and do the best he can for those he loves.

9   For most people, the most important creation is their own life. And in this life, the most blessed chapters are those in which they love and are loved in return.

10 There is no great literary creator whose work is primarily devoted to creating the immortal remembrance of family members he most loves—that is, unless we consider the characters of the *Tanach* as God's children.

11 In the beginning, God created out of love for the creation; the goal of the human creator should be to bring greater and greater goodness and blessing to the world.

12 Out of love of God and God's creation should come songs of praise.

13 When we create in strength and know that what we have done will bring joy and inspiration to others, we cannot help but feel great happiness, as *Hashem* created the world with a word, *light,* and saw that it was good.

⌘   ⌘   ⌘

55. FRUSTRATIONS OF CREATION

1   The rule of unintended consequences works both in the world of action and in the world of creation. Very often the creator strives to have a certain influence in

the world and achieves something contradictory. More often, there are consequences the creator has not imagined, both for good and for evil.

2   The creator strives to have the mastery of all skills, styles, forms, and genres in order to be like God in creation. In time, he discovers that, despite all his effort, most ways of working are simply not given to him.

3   The creator is misinterpreted; intentions are invented for him, statements are taken out of context. He is misread.

4   It is possible to give one's lifetime to a mistake. There are many who have devoted their lives to literary creation, only to have this amount to nothing.

5   There are those who prepare and wait all their life for one brief time of creation that will justify them forever. Others work all their lives for the moment that never comes.

6   The great creator supposes he has solved the problem for all time when he has formulated one response from a long tradition of responses to the problem.

7   In posterity, one may see the great creator as above his own time, while in his own time, he is seen as one among many.

8   There are creators who know their work is true and do not despair of it but despair of its power to change the lives they have damaged in being so devoted to their work.

9   No one is ever completely known as they want to be known. There are always misunderstandings. Even

praise of a certain kind can be a terrible insult for the creator.

10   The perpetual suspicion that the work of creation is vanity and not service of God must haunt those Jewish creators whose principal activity is not Torah study.

11   The creator, however great, is small beside those who have gone before and will come after. He is but one small voice in a universe of voices.

12   The work is always somehow different from what it was planned to be — often less — even though the struggle is made over and over again. Still, the highest level cannot be reached, and one is made to feel one's inherent limitation and inferiority not only before God but also before other human creators.

13   Understanding the value of one's own work when the world does not brings pain and frustration. The creator may spend years trying to reach the world and yet be continually misunderstood, continually disregarded and neglected. To strive to give and then not be accepted is a painful experience that most of those who strive to create know too well.

❖   ❖   ❖

56. REJECTION AND THE FORTUNATE FAILURE

1   Rejection often provides an opportunity for correction, which in turn makes a higher creation possible.

Rejection often provides us with the need for reconsideration, which leads to change and development in a new direction.

2 In later life, we often bless a failure that pained us greatly and was incomprehensible when it happened. A fortunate failure gives creation a dimension it never would have had if success had come too early or too easily.

3 Ideally, success that comes after repeated failure should prevent our having the arrogance of those who succeed too easily. It should teach us that success does not come simply by our own effort but requires the miraculous help of God.

④ The failure is fortunate when it delays the coming of a success that, had it come too early, would have destroyed the creator.

5 Rejection and suffering may provide the test of the creator's character through which he is strengthened for deeper work than he otherwise ever would have been capable of.

6 But isn't this whole concept of failure in creation alien to a Jewish tradition where anyone who learns serves God? Isn't it possible to think in terms of such failure only when one has a kind of ambition that in traditional Jewish religious terms is reprehensible?

7 In one sense, the true creator in the Jewish tradition always has a sense either of his own failure or his own smallness — his own humility — before the vastness of the tradition and the greatness of the Creator.

8 A failure may be fortunate if it enables the creator to delay addressing a problem until a later stage of life.

Then his additional experience and wisdom might enable him to provide a deeper solution than he might have provided when younger.

9   It might be argued that the long delay in allowing Jews to fully enter Western civilization helped them to have a power and maturity in learning that made their great contributions to it possible. With the people, too, failure at an early stage is a step in the process toward greater success later.

10   Failure may also be fortunate in that it might teach compassion and sympathy for others who do not succeed. It may also be of great assistance to the one who needs to teach others.

11   For generations there have been Jewish scholars who were failures in material terms but not in terms of their aspirations to serve God in the right way.

12   The creator who fails repeatedly may come to find in failure a secure home, an excuse for further failure. Thus failure misused can close the door on a life of creation, as success wisely appropriated can lead to new levels of creation.

13   If one judges oneself by the highest standard, one is always a failure. If one keeps in mind that one is God's creation, whose purpose is to serve the Creator, one is always doing what is right. The wise creator should understand that, beyond his own small effort, there is the creation of God, which is a joy in which to partake.

⊠   ⊠   ⊠

57. LONELINESS, SUFFERING, AND CREATION

1   In the Jewish tradition, suffering is not worshiped and pain is not glorified. Suffering is first and above all an evil. Yet it is clear that there is suffering that may contribute to personal redemption, suffering that provides an opportunity for greater devotion to and closeness to God. Out of our great pain and sorrow come the deepest prayers to God.

2   Those who have the deepest faith find in their disappointments yet another means of worshiping God.

3   The most powerful of all poetic pleas to God, the Psalms, illustrate how suffering leads the soul to greater closeness to God.

4   It is far easier for us to justify our sufferings (especially since we know our own sinful nature from inside) than it is understand the sufferings of those we love. The sufferings of those we love may also be the greatest inspiration for our turning to God in creation.

5   The creator must in some sense go where no one has gone before; he must go there alone, without help, and he must, in doing this, risk rejection, neglect, failure, and ridicule. Seeing what no one else has seen before, the creator often pays a price in suffering.

6   The creator is often able to understand what others will understand only after years of learning his work. He cannot accept but he can sense the painful truth that it may be only after he has died that his work will be properly understood. For a certain kind of creator, such failure in one's own time is nonetheless failure forever.

7   The creator is not privileged in being freed of ordinary human suffering. But he may be privileged in having the opportunity to give this suffering meaning in his work.

8   The Jews are the people who have created and suffered the most in history. This connection cannot be incidental only but must certainly relate to God's plan for us.

9   A paradise without suffering would not be a human paradise, for suffering comes of effort, and effort — including that which entails failure — is necessary for real creation.

10 The Jews are a people who dwell alone. The great creators, too, dwell alone, as God was alone in creating the world.

11 Suffering seems inherent in the process of creation itself, in which failure is more common than success, and few are chosen and many left out.

12 We suffer because we strive for something higher, and this striving sets us apart from others. Even in the striving to come near to God, we may see the price of daring to leave the many behind.

13 The suffering of the creator comes out of the great demands he makes of himself. He may understand these as special demands that God imposes upon him.

▨   ▨   ▨

58. STRIVING FOR GREATNESS IN CREATION

1   The striving for greatness in creation is the striving to be chosen by God. It is the striving to be chosen from the many would-be great creators. It is the striving to have one's loved ones live in human remembrance. It is the striving to be part of the mind of God forever.

2   Of the billions of people who live in this world now, there are a few hundred who will be part of the cultural heritage of mankind in distant generations. There are overwhelming odds against any specific individual's being chosen for greatness. Such a choice must be made by God; for most of us, the moral meaning of such a choice is not clear.

3   The lives of the great are no less filled with disappointment than the lives of others. Greatness and happiness are not necessarily one. There is even the claim that it is only some special suffering that qualifies the great for their task of supreme dedication in work.

4   The fact that in cultural creation the great provide a gift of entertainment and instruction to mankind for generations does, in some way, hint at the moral and religious meaning of such creation. Many works of secular literature do broaden the human capacity for enjoying this world; they do bring a kind of goodness to the world, even if that goodness at times seems in contradiction to religious spirit and teaching.

5   There is a greatness that seems to come inadvertently as if, in the course of living for other things, the creator saw his work transformed into something greater than he had imagined. The work of Shakespeare can, in some sense, be seen in this way.

6   The prophets do not strive for their own name or greatness. They strive to serve God.

7   In the striving for greatness there is pride and sin, the desire to be chosen and exalted above others. Yet in the Jewish tradition, the very greatest are those who are most humble, who seem almost chosen against their will to do a service God demands of them.

8   God chose not the strongest, not the most powerful, but the smallest and most humble of peoples to be His messenger to mankind. This underlines that the source of human greatness is not in humanity itself but in what is beyond us.

9   Why, then, does the individual human being strive for his own greatness, when he knows there is only one Source of Greatness, One Judge who will determine whose work will live and whose will not? Is it that the individual — even the individual Jew — is not content to be chosen as part of a people but seeks special love and approval from God? Is the striving for greatness in this sense connected most deeply with the need to be specially chosen and loved by God?

10 The striving for greatness is the striving to come as close to God as possible in one's power of creation. This impulse can contain within it both the desire to serve God and resentment at the One one we will never approach in greatness.

11 The great person is often the one who discovers for mankind some truth it has not known before or

creates for it a work that provides a recurrent source of joy and insight. In serving mankind, the truly great person serves God, whether or not that is his intention.

12 The commentators and interpreters are in the eyes of the Jewish tradition less great than the biblical figures whose stories they interpret. And the commentators who come after these commentators are still less great. And the tradition is the more distant the generation from Sinai, the more diminished its power of creation.

13 It is possible that those who are unknown to humanity as a whole and have no great name of their own are greatest in God's judgment.

⊠   ⊠   ⊠

59. CREATION AND LITERARY GREATNESS

1 Better a single masterpiece than a thousand forgotten works. It is remarkable how the greatness of many is made by a single work.

2 The rule is that most great creators are recognized in their own time, not necessarily with the same weight of recognition that posterity gives them. But then, literary greatness is in some sense defined as survival through generations. Many who are great in their own time cease to be great a short while after.

3 Must the religious Jew, in judging literary creations, divide the world into two distinct categories: those

who are closest to God in works of Torah literature and those whose fundamental thrust — whether or not they are Jewish — is not in direct relation to Torah? For the religious Jew, must this second category — however powerful aesthetically — always contain works of lesser value than the first?

4 For many, Shakespeare was the greatest of human creators because he created the most intensely poetic and humanly diverse of all imaginary worlds.

5 Most great creators have one period of time when they do their greatest works. For poets it is in their youth; for novelists, middle age; for philosophers, old age. This contrasts with the Torah scholar, whose creation lasts the length of his life and, ideally, grows in power with age.

6 At the highest level of creation there is no competition; each work is a world of its own.

7 There are great literary figures — the Baal Shem Tov in our tradition and Socrates in that of Western philosophy — whose legend is created for them, whose works are written for them by others (usually their students and disciples).

8 The greatest and most influential of all literary works is one whose aim is not primarily aesthetic. The greatest of all works of literature is more than literature; it is the supreme work of religion and morality.

9 Every great work is in time transformed by the readings of successive generations. Every great work becomes greater through the books it has inspired the writing of. Every great book is the subject of com-

mentaries that in time develop its meaning beyond
that which its original creator conceived.

10 The great work is the one in which each successive
generation of humanity can find its own eternal truth.

11 The greatest literary creations are not improved by
those who learn its techniques and use them as a
formula for creating new works. Each great literary
creation (unless scientific and technological) in a sense
stands on its own.

12 Today the tradition of literary greatness in the
Western world is largely defined in the academic
world. And here, too, the struggles over curriculum
are political and historical ones in which great literature is defined in terms of the interests of its readers.
This academic world is both a temptation and a
contradiction, as well as an expansion in meaning for
the traditional Jewish way of reading literature.

13 The greatest of all literary works is the one given by
God to the people of Israel as their sacred Scripture.

                    ▩   ▩   ▩

60. THE IDEAL LITERARY CREATION:
TANACH

1   The ideal literary creation serves God's purpose in
history and is God's revelation to mankind.

2   The ideal literary creation provides a guide to life and
an understanding of how we are to act if we are to

sanctify life. It is the world's basic book of ethics and morality.

3   The ideal literary creation convinces us of the miraculous power of the Creator. It provides us with an understanding of how mankind is to walk in God's ways of freedom and dignity.

4   The ideal literary creation expresses the deepest needs of the human heart. It expresses the longing for God and for justice.

5   The ideal literary creation presents mankind with an ideal of what it is to be in this world.

6   The ideal literary creation expresses the full range of feelings and situations in life. It is the story of the human heart, which can be relived by generation after generation of readers.

7   The ideal literary creation speaks to what is eternal in the human situation.

8   The ideal literary creation tells the story of God's relation to mankind and to the Jewish people.

9   The ideal literary creation is an anthology of forms and situations and reveals to us the best and the worst in human character and dreams.

10   The ideal literary creation reveals the truth of life, of human conflict and struggle. It reveals how good and evil continually struggle within us and in the world for predominance and power.

11   The ideal literary creation presents a hope of redemption and the path of salvation for mankind.

12   The ideal literary creation is a sacred work, the study of which elevates the soul.

13   The ideal literary creation teaches how to sanctify our lives by living in accordance with the teachings of God. It teaches us how to walk in the way of the Creator and sanctify our own lives in creation.

About the Author

Shalom (Seymour) Freedman is a Jewish writer who has worked for many years in Israel. The recipient of a Ph.D. in English and American Literature from Cornell University, he has contributed to the *Encyclopedia of Judaism*, the *Zionist Press Service*, the *Jerusalem Post*, local Jerusalem newspapers, and a variety of other publications. He has published two previous books, *Seven Years in Israel* and a book of poems, *Mourning for My Father*. An essential element of his *aliyah* has been his devotion to Jewish learning in houses of study in the Holy City.